Vagabond Two Vagabond Two Vagabond Two Vag

Freudian Slips

The Casualties of Psychoanalysis from the Wolf Man to Marilyn Monroe

By Luciano Mecacci

Translated by Allan Cameron

Vagabond Voices
Sulaisiadar 'san Rudha

Translation copyright © Vagabond Voices Publishing Ltd 2009

First published in Italian as *Il caso Marilyn M. e altri disastri della psicoanalisi* © Giuseppe Laterza & Figli 2000, Rome-Bari

Vagabond Voices Publishing Ltd.
3 Sulaisiadar
An Rubha
Eilean Leòdhais / Isle of Lewis
Alba / Scotland HS2 0PU

ISBN 978-0-9560560-1-6

Printed and bound by Thomson Litho, East Kilbride

For further information on Vagabond Voices, see the website, www.vagabondvoices.co.uk

This Freud of ours is a great man, but more for novelists than for the sick (Grande uomo quel nostro Freud, ma più per i romanzieri che per gli ammalati) – Italo Svevo

Contents

Preface

In *Master and Margarita*, Mikhail Bulgakov describes "Satan's grand ball" in which men and women, overcome by Eros, allow Death to embrace them. They dance naked, scream, throw themselves in a swimming pool filled with champagne, and then vanish into oblivion. The ball, which lasts through the night, is attended by "kings, counts, knights, suicidal maniacs, poisoners, the dead by hanging, madams, torturers, swindlers, hangmen, informers, traitors, lunatics, spies and rapists."

The ball that I am going to speak of has lasted for a century. We have all been witnesses and spectators – occasionally sceptical, sometimes indifferent and often enthusiastic. The dancing party has been made up of psychoanalysts and their patients.

Psychoanalysts came up with a new understanding of the human soul and a new therapy to treat it. They gradually established some principles and ground rules to govern relationships with their patients, and these mainly concerned the possible development of emotional ties during analysis on the part of the patient, the analyst or both. All this presupposed that analysts would acquire such maturity and psychological stability that they could control their own emotions, but this is not what occurred, and in spite of official reassurances from representatives of the psychoanalytical community, many alarming facts have emerged in recent years. It is not the intention of this book to be sensationalist in its treatment of a complex subject, and I hope, by adopting a historical perspective based on the disturbing biographies of the founders of psychoanalysis, to present an alternative overview of one of the most important cultural movements of the twentieth century.

We shall now take to the dance floor and see what happens.

Chapter 1
Marilyn M: power and celebrity clash on the couch

Strictly speaking, the case of Marilyn Monroe is not a psychoanalytical one. Genuine cases of psychoanalysis are made public by psychoanalysts who often write up the case histories and explain the methods of analysis used and relations with their patients. Marilyn, on the other hand, was an artistic, sociological, criminological and even political *cause célèbre*, but no psychoanalyst ever wrote about her.

Norma Jeane, who was born in Los Angeles on 1 June 1926, took the name Marilyn Monroe in 1946. That decision, taken at the very beginning of her acting career, also revealed her desire for a new identity. As Marilyn was to recall in her memoirs, a few years earlier she had felt herself divided into two personalities:

> I was full of a strange feeling, as if I were two people. One of them was Norma Jeane from the orphanage who belonged to nobody. The other was someone whose name I didn't know. But I knew where she belonged. She belonged to the ocean and the sky and the whole world...

When she wandered the streets of Manhattan or Santa Monica without make-up and wearing a black wig to avoid being recognised, Marilyn also used the name Zelda Zonk. Up until her marriage at the age of sixteen to James (Jim) Dougherty, Marilyn's life had consisted of a succession of moves from one adoptive family to another, and from the age of nine to eleven she found herself in a Los Angeles orphanage. She protested that she was not an orphan and that she

1

could have lived with her mother who was still alive, but to no avail. Marilyn had not yet understood that her mother, Gladys, was mentally ill and had been put in a psychiatric hospital. Gladys's diagnoses varied from manic-depressive psychosis to schizophrenia, and she too was on the move – from one hospital to another, as she switched between periods of lucidity and periods of madness in which she made several attempts at suicide. Gladys's mother, Della, had also suffered from manic-depressive psychosis and died in a psychiatric hospital. A few days before her death, she had tried to suffocate her granddaughter Marilyn with a cushion. The list goes on: the first husband of Marilyn's grandmother, who finished his days in a psychiatric hospital, or the equally tragic end of Della's father (Marilyn's great-grandfather), who committed suicide. There were other sad and no less devastating events in Marilyn's childhood. At the age of eight, she was sexually abused by an actor who was lodging at her home. At eleven, it was the turn of a new "daddy" in one of her many adoptive families. At fifteen she was again abused by an older cousin.

Her first marriage, to Jim, freed Marilyn from the nightmare of adoptive families and the possibility of being returned to an orphanage. It was also her first encounter with a protective male figure. Her father had not married her mother when she became pregnant, and never acknowledged the daughter who attempted to contact him on several occasions. However, Marilyn found substitute mother-figures in her various "adoptive" mothers and, when she became an actress, in her female colleagues and assistants. Jim, who was five years her senior, described the personality of his very young wife in great detail:

I was very much in love. She had a quick wit and a beautiful face and body. She was the most mature sixteen-year-old I had ever met when we married... There was something mature and terribly proper about her, which she may have inherited. I later noticed this trait in her mother, even though she was emotionally disturbed. Then at other times she was like a little girl. She had had no childhood and it showed. There were two Norma Jeanes - one was the child whose dolls and stuffed animals were propped up on top of the chest of drawers "so they can see what's going on." The other Norma Jeane had moods in her that were unpredictable and often a little scary. You'd catch glimpses of someone who had been unloved for too long, unwanted for too many years.

For years Marilyn suffered from a stammer, a disorder that appeared during her stay in the orphanage, probably after the first case of sexual abuse. That stammer, a symptom of her insecurity, never went away. Even when she was a well-established actress, it would reveal itself during the filming of particularly difficult scenes or in other tense situations. On occasions she would suffer from vomiting, typically before starting a radio transmission or interview. Even more serious were her nightmares, which also started while she was in the orphanage. David Conover, who was her friend in the forties, told of how he was woken by Marilyn's screams in the middle of the night. Marilyn was sitting on the bed shaking and covered in sweat:

> "It's that n-nightmare," she stammered. "What happened?" he asked. "They force me into a straitjacket and carry me out of the house. I'm screaming, 'I'm not crazy! I'm not crazy!' When we come to a brick bu-building that looks like my old

orphanage, we go through one black iron door after another and each door slams shut behind me. 'I don't belong here!' I shout. 'What are you doing to me?' They pu-put me in a bleak room with barred windows and they go out and lock the iron door, leaving me in a straitjacket. 'I don't belong here!' I scream again and again, until I have no more breath."

In another of her recurring dreams, Marilyn would run naked through a cemetery at dawn trying to find the way out. When she woke up, she would retain a vivid image of the graves she had passed and the dew-laden grass on which she had run barefoot. Marilyn's last housekeeper, Eunice Murray, recalled that, even during the final part of her life, she frequently suffered from nightmares. Shortly after falling asleep, Marilyn would wake up with a scream, shaking from head to foot and covered in sweat. She would get out of bed and sit in a chair until she calmed down.

Marilyn was noted for her bizarre or abnormal behaviour, especially her persistent lateness in getting to the set. Like all actresses, she was supposed to get up early for make-up and dressing so that she would be ready for shooting around eight or nine in the morning. However, she often turned up around midday, confused by medication for insomnia or anxiety. On other occasions, she wouldn't even put in an appearance, thus causing considerable delays in the production of the film, and constant misunder-standings and quarrels with the studio, the director and the other actors.

Marilyn did not take great care of her possessions. Because of her nomadic lifestyle, she may not have ever developed any concept of what it would be like to have a stable home where objects could be kept safe and used to hand down a family's historical memory.

Her room was piled up with clothes, of which there were many, although they were 'simple', as Lena Pepitone, her New York housekeeper, remembered:

> Black and brown velvet pants, many pairs of identical black and white checked pants, beige and white cotton and silk blouses, an endless array of spaghetti-strap dresses with plunging necklines, and a shoe store of flat Ferragamo shoes. She owned four mink coats, in brown and white, a lot of scarves – but, of course, no underwear at all. In the bathroom vanity, she stored bottles and bottles of her favorite perfume, Chanel No. 5, along with the more expensive Joy. But rarely did she ever perfume herself, let alone bathe or shower.

It was also common knowledge that Marilyn felt most at ease when she was naked: she wandered around the house and garden without clothes, she slept with nothing on and spurned the use of underpants. As an adolescent, the naked body was one of her recurring dreams:

> I dreamed that I was standing up in a church without any clothes on, and all the people there were lying at my feet on the floor of the church, and I walked naked, with a sense of freedom, over their prostrate forms, being careful not to step on anyone.
>
> My impulse to appear naked and my dreams about it had no shame or sense of sin in them. Dreaming of people looking at me made me feel less lonely. I think I wanted them to see me naked because I was ashamed of the clothes I wore – the never-changing faded blue dress of poverty. Naked, I was like the other girls...

Occasionally this nudity, a source of admiration because of her beauty, embarrassed those who were acquainted with her personal habits: she would lie naked on her bed, drinking champagne and eating veal cutlets, and then clean her greasy fingers on the sheets covered with scraps of food. Given that Marilyn used neither pants nor sanitary towels, her sheets became a problem during menstruation. "You see," her housekeeper would point out, "Marilyn didn't like sanitary napkins any more than she liked bathtubs." These were not Marilyn's only irritating habits. Lena Pepitone was to recall, "Whatever and wherever she ate, etiquette never concerned Marilyn. Among her unpleasant habits were incessant belching and farting." She considered this behaviour completely natural, and found the discomfort of her fellow-diners very amusing.

The woman who for most people was the very embodiment of sexuality and a symbol of the libido, and who was presented as such in films, photographs and interviews, in reality conducted a sex life that was complex to say the very least. Not only did she have three husbands (the seaman James Dougherty, the baseball legend Joe DiMaggio and the writer Arthur Miller, and perhaps even a fourth one for a few days, the journalist Robert Slatzer), but she also had relationships with many famous performers, such as Marlon Brando, Elia Kazan, Yves Montand and Frank Sinatra; nor did she spurn men who had no celebrity status. Her relationship with the Kennedys merits a section on its own. These affairs did not enjoy any form of "exclusivity", as was well-known to journalists and biographers, who often went on the trail of the clandestine encounters that Marilyn plotted with one or other of her lovers while "officially" committed to Jim, Joe or Arthur. In some cases, these took on extreme forms, such as the orgy in which Marilyn is supposed to have been filmed taking part in more than one sex act in the presence of Sinatra and the mafia boss Sam Giancana.

Her reckless sex life was accompanied by a overriding desire for motherhood. The miscarriages she suffered threw her into a state of profound depression, which only alcohol and drugs managed to alleviate. Then there was the controversial tale (told by Donald H. Wolfe) of the daughter Marilyn is supposed to have had by John F. Kennedy in November 1947. The story is that the child was taken away from her in order to prevent a serious scandal that could have compromised the promising career of the future president of the United States. Marilyn is supposed to have referred to this daughter on rare occasions, sometimes to bemoan her stolen motherhood and sometimes to threaten JFK and later Robert F. Kennedy.

This was the background to one of the great cinema actresses, whose psychological state was however as fragile as her fame. Marilyn's mental instability was subjected to almost all forms of therapy: orthodox analytical treatment (through words and transference, à la Freud), psychotropic drugs in massive doses, straitjackets and internment in a mental hospital. To put it another way, if words were not enough, then drugs were used, and if these proved insufficient to calm her state of mind, there was always physical restraint.

Marilyn was treated by five psychoanalysts: Margaret Herz Hohenberg, Anna Freud, Marianne Rie Kris, Ralph S. Greenson and Milton Wexler. Psychoanalysis was fashionable in Hollywood at the time that Marilyn started out on her acting career. Actors, actresses and directors were in analysis with famous psychoanalysts who lived in the wealthiest parts of Los Angeles: Hollywood, Beverly Hills and Santa Monica. As Stephen Farber and Marc Green demonstrated in their book *Hollywood on the Couch* (with the equally suggestive subtitle: *A Candid Look at the Overheated Love Affair between Psychiatrists and Moviemakers*), psychoanalysts held important positions within the cinema world, to the point where they became advisers to the studios and consultants for the scripting of films that increasingly depicted the psychoanalyst struggling to overcome the anguish of the psyche. It was Lee Strasberg, her teacher in performing arts at the Actors Studio, who advised Marilyn to go into analysis. The method that she was learning, according to the reasoning that Lee provided, would not have been effective if she didn't unlock the emotions that lay hidden in her unconscious. The "method", as it came to be called, was based on the principle that actors could only produce a wide range of emotional states once they had been able to link these to their own emotional histories and relationships.

So in February 1955, having just turned twenty-nine, Marilyn started her sessions with Margaret Herz Hohenberg, who had been suggested to her by her photographer friend, Milton Greene. Greene had also undergone analysis with Hohenberg, an immigrant of Hungarian origin who had become a psychoanalyst after having studied medicine in Vienna, Budapest and Prague, and had moved to New York in 1939. Marilyn had frequent sessions with her: three, four and even five times a week. At the same time, Marilyn used drugs to alleviate her anxiety and overcome her insomnia.

In July 1956 Marilyn came to London to film *The Prince and the Showgirl*, directed by Laurence Olivier, who also had a leading role. Marilyn's lateness on set, her lack of concentration and her sudden mood swings caused considerable problems with the progress of the film. According to the most recent biography of Marilyn written by Donald H. Wolfe, the actress had again secretly met up with JFK in London, and shortly afterwards her marriage to Arthur Miller began to break down. Wolfe discovered a hand-written note in which Miller agreed with the opinion expressed by Olivier that Marilyn was a "whore". The actress fell into a state of profound depression, and so Hohenberg was asked to fly from New York to London to re-establish the psychological stability of her patient, thus allowing filming to continue. The psychoanalyst managed to calm her down, but before returning to her practice in New York, she advised Marilyn to continue her analysis with Anna Freud.

Hence the thirty-year-old Marilyn started a new relationship under analysis with none other than the daughter of Sigmund Freud. In 1956, Anna was sixty-one. The housekeeper at the Freud household, Paula Fichtl, remembers the first time that Marilyn came round for analysis – she appeared in a black Rolls-Royce. Marilyn "was wearing a plain blue gabardine with its collar up. She was wearing no make-up. Her platinum blond hair was covered by a soft hat, and her large dark sunglasses rendered her almost unrecognizable." Marilyn went to No. 20 Maresfield Gardens every day, and gradually she regained her serenity. Anna Freud had her visit the nursery school at the Hampstead Clinic and Marilyn played with the children. Anna Freud put Marilyn through the marbles test: she put marbles on the table in front of Marilyn, who then had to move them. Anna interpreted the way in which she did this. What did Marilyn do? She shifted the marbles one after the other towards Anna who could then diagnose "a desire for sexual contact". Marilyn's clinical file, held with Anna Freud's papers, summarises the diagnosis as follows:

> Emotionally unstable, highly impulsive, and needing continuous approval from the outside world; she cannot bear solitude and tends to get depressed when faced with rejection; paranoid with schizophrenic elements.

Within a fortnight, Marilyn had managed to recover and return to work on the film. After a few months, the actress was prepared to express her gratitude to Anna Freud with a large cheque. When she was back in New York however, Marilyn wanted to change her analyst and it was Anna Freud who suggested Marianne Rie Kris. Kris was not only a friend of Freud's daughter, but also of Lee Strasberg, Marilyn's famous acting teacher, and his wife Paula. Marilyn's friends, the Strasbergs, lived in the same apartment block as Kris. Marianne Rie Kris, who became the actress's analyst in March 1957, was another prominent figure in the history of psychoanalysis. Born in Vienna in 1900, she was the daughter of Oskar Rie, doctor to the Freud family and Sigmund's constant partner at cards. Her mother, Melanie, was the sister of Ida Bondy, Wilhelm Fliess's wife. Fliess was a great friend and correspondent of Sigmund, and furthermore had been a patient of Josef Breuer, who had worked with Sigmund on his *Studies on Hysteria*. Marianne, who graduated in medicine in Vienna in 1925, had undergone analysis with Franz Alexander in Berlin (Alexander had in turn been analysed by Hanns Sachs, one of Sigmund Freud's earliest pupils). When she returned to Vienna, Marianne completed her analysis with Sigmund Freud, who used to call her his "adoptive daughter". She had also been supervised by Anna, who had played with her during her childhood. She married Ernst Kris, the art historian and psychoanalyst (Ernst had been in analysis under

Helene Deutsch, who in turn had been analysed by Sigmund). Their son Anton was analysed by John M. Murray, the husband of Eunice, Marilyn's last housekeeper (we will be returning to the Murrays as a couple). This intricate network of kinships, friendships and relationships between analysts and patients is illustrated in Fig. 1, in relation to Kris's "constellation". (Of course, each constellation has one or more connections with other constellations, and the reader will easily be able to identify these links in later diagrams.)

Marilyn took up with Kris where Hohenberg had left off, with as many as five sessions a week. The purpose of analysis was to delve deeply into the past, to bring past traumas back to the surface, and to confront maternal and paternal figures who had been absent. Marilyn was constantly taken back to her childhood, a fictitious childhood that caused her further insecurity and anxiety. But this was not all. When the sessions with Kris were over, Marilyn would take the lift to the next floor up where her acting instructor Lee Strasberg was waiting for her. He never failed to subject her to further stressful exercises in emotional identification with people from her childhood who reminded her of her unhappy past (do a starving child, now do a dejected orphan, etc.). It is hardly surprising that Marilyn turned to drugs after these exhausting sessions in which, first as a patient and then as an actress, she was taken back to a childhood she had wanted to escape from through fame and fortune.

Marilyn broke off her analysis with Kris when she returned to Los Angeles to act in *Let's Make Love* together with Yves Montand. At the beginning of 1960, Marilyn suffered a serious psychological crisis, which was thought to have been caused by the end of her brief love affair with Montand. But, according to her biographer Donald H. Wolfe, Marilyn was shaken by the announcement from JFK that he was going to run for the White House: this destroyed any illusions about her being able to marry him because the future president, supposing he had ever nurtured such intentions, would no longer be able to divorce Jacqueline.

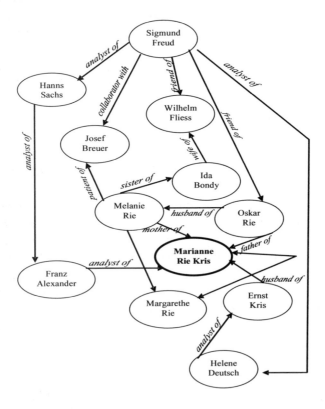

Fig. 1. The Marianne Rie Kris constellation. This constellation reappears in Chapter 7 as part of an even more complex network (Fig. 6), and is connected with other constellations illustrated in later diagrams for one or more of its members.

Kris asked Ralph S. Greenson to help Marilyn, and in January 1960 Marilyn started a new course of psychoanalysis with Greenson, one of the most famous analysts in Los Angeles. Greenson was not only well known in Hollywood's film circles, but also in those of psychoanalytical research and amongst the most respected psychiatric practices. He was born in Brooklyn in 1911 of Russian-Jewish immigrants, whose surname was Greenschpoon. The father, who had a passion for Shakespeare, called his twins Romeo and Juliet after the names of the two young lovers destined for a tragic death. Romeo decided first to change his forename to Ralph – perhaps in order to avoid embarrassment and teasing amongst friends when he introduced himself and his sister: "We're Romeo and Juliet, and we're twins," – and then his surname to Greenson in 1937. While Juliet studied music and became an excellent professional pianist, Ralph commenced his medical studies at Columbia University and he finished them at Berne in Switzerland in 1934. There, Ralph met and married Hildegard Troesch (called Hildi) in 1935, and they had two children, Daniel (later to become a psychiatrist) and Joan. After having worked in a Los Angeles hospital from 1934 to 1938, he returned to Europe and underwent analysis in Vienna with Wilhelm Stekel, who had been analysed by Sigmund Freud (Stekel is a name that will recur several times in this book). Having returned to Los Angeles, he started analysis in 1938 with Otto Fenichel. In 1942 he was enrolled in the United States army and worked as a medical officer at a hospital for veterans close to New York. In 1943 he was in a serious accident while travelling in a military ambulance, which caused a skull fracture with neurological consequences that were to manifest themselves many years later (in his biography of Marilyn, Donald Spoto described these as epileptic fits, a lack of motor coordination and a complete loss of his sense of smell). He was subsequently exempted from taking part in the war overseas and was put in charge of the neuropsychiatric unit at the Fort Logan military hospital in Colorado. Captain Greenson devoted his energies to treating soldiers suffering psychiatric disorders caused by the war. His dedication and commitment to their rehabilitation and return to society were described in a novel written by his friend Leo Rosten, entitled *Captain Newman, M.D.* The book was turned into a film of the same name in 1963, and Gregory Peck played the lead role.

When he demobbed in 1946, he started a psychiatric and psychoanalytical practice in Los Angeles. Later he was made professor of psychiatry at the University of Los Angeles and was one of the most authoritative members of the Institute of Psychoanalysis of Los Angeles. Greenson, a fascinating man, was liked by everyone: by Anna Freud, with whom he corresponded over a long period of time (he was one of the select few who could call her "Anna" and speak to her on intimate terms), by Hollywood actors and actresses (apart from Marilyn, his patients included Frank Sinatra, Tony Curtis and Vivien Leigh), by producers and directors (who asked his advice and professional opinion) and by the wider public (for whom he wrote articles in layman's language and held extremely accessible and well-attended conferences on popular subjects). His evenings of highly polished chamber music held in his Santa Monica home brought together famous and important Hollywood figures: writers, politicians, and leading psychoanalysts and academics in the field of humanities. The producer Tamar Simon Hofs recalled that "That's the only analytic 'salon' I can think of in which there was fun. You knew you'd always meet a cross-section of people – Anna Freud, Margaret Mead [the well-known anthropologist], Masters and Johnson [the two well-known experts on sexual behaviour], plus lots of Hollywood people. The talk at the place was fabulous."

Greenson was considered one of the people best placed to faithfully interpret classical Freudian psychoanalysis, which was founded on the "art of interpretation and the ability to relate to another human being", as he asserted in his basic work, *The Technique and Practice of Psychoanalysis.*

However, the psychiatrist backed up his psychoanalytical technique with drug therapy, which he prescribed to Marilyn on a massive scale. Another doctor, Hyman Engelberg, whom Greenson himself had recommended to Marilyn, was also prescribing her psychotropic drugs. In the end they divided out their tasks: Greenson treated Marilyn with words and Engelberg treated her with drugs. While such drugs were widely used in film circles, they had never been used in the quantities that Marilyn took. According to Spoto, Greenson was responsible for prescribing her with 300 milligrams of Nembutal per night (when the maximum dose for insomnia was 100 for two weeks).

Marilyn significantly increased her reliance on drugs during the filming of *The Misfits* in 1960. A situation in which the director John Huston was plagued by gambling debts, Clark Gable had health problems and Montgomery Clift was acting strangely, was always likely to cause Marilyn to have a serious nervous breakdown, and it threatened to destroy her. The drugs prescribed by Engelberg (and indirectly by Greenson) reduced her to a state of confusion, and she needed to be treated in a Los Angeles clinic to get over it, while filming was temporarily suspended.

Marilyn was extremely impressed by Greenson's charisma when she first met her new psychoanalyst in January 1960. She went to him when she was on the Californian coast, and continued her analysis with Kris when she was back in New York. Marilyn immediately told her New York housekeeper, Lena Pepitone, of her enthusiasm for Greenson, and Pepitone recalled the following telephone conversation:

"Lena, Lena, I've finally found him. I've found a Jesus for myself!" "A Jesus?" [Lena asked]. "Yes, Lena. I call him Jesus. He's doing wonderful things for me." "What?" [Lena inquired] "What does he do?"... "He gives me courage. He makes me smart, makes me think. I can face anything with him. I'm not scared anymore."

At this stage, Greenson and Kris started to write to each other about Marilyn, and this correspondence continued even after the actress's death. Greenson informed Kris that he had detected symptoms of paranoia and schizophrenia. In one letter he wrote that, "as she [Marilyn] becomes more anxious, she begins to act like an orphan, a waif, and she masochistically provokes [people] to mistreat her and to take advantage of her." Lena Pepitone also claimed that as fragments of her past history came out, "she began to talk more and more about the traumatic experience of an 'orphan child'."

Psychoanalytical circles were to discuss Marilyn's case for a long time, but in a manner that never allowed the facts and their opinions to become known outside their closed world, which was always very good at protecting its members' secrets. Anna Freud's housekeeper, Paula, remembered an episode from August 1959: "The Greensons were put up in my room, indeed the doctor slept in my bed. Miss Freud spent many hours discussing the Miss Monroe case with the gentleman doctor and with Doctor Kris." Hence Marilyn's biographers, who have examined every detail of her relationship with Greenson almost on a daily basis, failed to notice that the Californian psychoanalyst knew about Marilyn's condition before she started to undergo analysis with him. As we shall see, Greenson already knew many things about Marilyn, and he was not interested in Marilyn simply as a clinical case.

When she went back to New York at the end of 1960, during the preparation of the divorce from Arthur Miller, Marilyn returned to her sessions with Kris, but also spent a great deal of time on the phone to Greenson, who was in Los Angeles. In January 1961, she drew up a will in which she left a not inconsiderable legacy to Kris. Yet another divorce, the death of Clark Gable and the failure of *The Misfits* were terrible blows for Marilyn, who spent her days sleeping in a darkened room, stuffed with tranquillisers, only leaving the house to go to Kris for analysis. On 5 February, Kris decided that Marilyn needed treatment in the Psychiatric Department of New York Hospital. She was locked in a padded cell, and her nightmare had come true. Marilyn screamed and battered the door with her fists. In the end, she managed to smash the window of the door with a chair. The more she repeated this behaviour, the more she was considered mad and deserving of a straitjacket. During the night, as Marilyn later recalled, there was a continuous procession of doctors and nurses who went to look at the famous actress: "There I was, with my arms bound. I was not able to defend myself. I was a curiosity piece, with no one who had my interest at heart.". She was diagnosed as "extremely disturbed" and "potentially self-destructive".

After three days, Marilyn managed to get a note out through a nurse for the Strasbergs, in which she desperately pleaded for help:

> Dear Lee and Paula,
> Dr. Kris has put me in the hospital under the care of idiot doctors. They both should not be my doctors. I'm locked up with these poor nutty people. I'm sure to end up a nut too if I stay in this nightmare. Please help me. This is the last place I should be. I love you both.
>
> Marilyn
> P.S. I'm on the dangerous floor. It's like a cell.

The Strasbergs contacted Joe DiMaggio, who had stayed very close to Marilyn. The ex-husband, who was still in love with her, rushed from Florida to New York to demand that Marilyn be released immediately. As he was told that they would need Kris's permission, Joe telephoned the psychoanalyst and threatened that he would destroy the hospital brick by brick if Marilyn was not allowed to leave. When she was eventually taken out of the hospital, Marilyn started to berate Kris violently during the drive home. Marilyn's masseur, Ralph Roberts, who went with Kris to collect her from the hospital, said:

> She was like a hurricane unleashed. I don't think Dr. Kris had ever seen her like that, and she was frightened and very shaken... Dr Kris was trembling and kept repeating over and over, "I did a terrible thing, a terrible thing. Oh, God, I didn't mean to. I didn't mean to, but I did."

That was the last time Marilyn saw Kris, who remained however one of the beneficiaries of her will. Joe realised the serious nature of Marilyn's psychological state and managed to persuade her to seek treatment at the Neurological Institute at Columbia

University, in the Presbyterian Hospital Medical Center. Marilyn was treated there from 10 February to 5 March 1961. Shortly after leaving this clinic, Marilyn wrote a long letter to Greenson (first published in Spoto's biography of 1993). In it, she described the psychological and physical violence she had been subjected to, and pointed out how doctors were only interested in their patients in as much as their disorders corresponded to those they had read about in textbooks, and not because they saw "life-suffering human being[s]".

After a short holiday in Florida with Joe DiMaggio, Marilyn returned to Los Angeles at the end of April 1961, where she resumed her sessions with Greenson. Initially there were two or three a week, but then the sessions became more frequent (not just one a day, but even twice a day for four or five hours without a break, not to mention the endless telephone calls). Marilyn had almost become a member of the Greenson family. She stopped for lunch with them, and often did the washing-up once lunch was over. She also became friendly with the two children: she talked about make-up and boys with Joan, who she taught to dance the twist, and about politics with Daniel.

Greenson's was another adoptive family, on a par with the ones that Marilyn had belonged to since her earliest childhood. Greenson's influence on Marilyn's life became increasingly dominant: he was a presence not only when she was undergoing analysis, but also in her daily life. He advised her, and he told her what she could not do. For example, it appears from a letter he sent to Kris in May 1961 that Greenson was opposed to her relationship with Frank Sinatra, a casual affair like so many others, but full of emotional resonance and conflict. However, as Wolfe points out in his biography, Greenson was not hostile to her continuing relationship with the president of the United States, one that was public knowledge in Hollywood circles. I will examine his motives later in the chapter.

One of the most interesting examples of Greenson's influence on Marilyn concerned the vicissitudes of the film on Freud directed by John Huston, up to its release in 1962. From the moment of the film's conception, the main obstacle was the categorical opposition of Freud's daughter Anna, who lamented "not being able to protect one's own father against becoming a film hero." There were long legal negotiations between the Freud family and the film's producers. In the end, the script written by Jean-Paul Sartre was replaced by another version that was slighter and less demanding. This one was the work of Charles Kaufman, whose meeting in London with Anna Freud was arranged by Greenson. Kaufman realised that Freud's daughter would never give her consent: "The idea of an actor putting on a false beard and impersonating the great man in her life would never be acceptable to her." Some of Anna's letters contain harsh and resentful comments on the film. In the end, it was Montgomery Clift who played the part of Sigmund Freud.

The director wanted to give Marilyn the part of Freud's patient "Cäcilie M." (Anna von Lieben), but the actress did not accept because of the pressures put on her by Greenson, who in turn had been persuaded by Anna Freud. This part was eventually given to Susannah York. It would have been a heavy blow for an earnest woman like Anna to have to watch the empty-headed Marilyn in a transference relationship with none other than her father and therapist. Who knows if she knew that Montgomery Clift, who was to play the part of that father and therapist, was having a homosexual relationship with his own analyst (as Farber and Green have pointed out)? Another aspect of the film was that it concerned the period of Sigmund Freud's friendship with Wilhelm Fliess, a relationship which was too deep and intimate not to suggest at least some latent homosexual element (something that even Freud recognised, for example in his letter of 6 October 1910 to Sandor Ferenczi).

In November 1961, Greenson advised Marilyn to take on a capable and experienced housekeeper to stay permanently with her, and he sent her Eunice Murray. No one who saw a lot of Marilyn in the last few months before her death liked Eunice. She jealously guarded Marilyn's life and interfered in everything she did. Marilyn's make-up artist, Whitey Snyder, noted that she was "a very strange lady. She was put into Marilyn's life by Greenson, and she was always whispering – whispering and listening. She was this constant presence, reporting everything back to Greenson." Eunice had been married to John M. Murray, but was divorced. They had built a grand Mexican-style house in Santa Monica, which had later been sold to Greenson.

In January 1962, Marilyn bought a house (also in Mexican style like that of the Greensons) in Fifth Helena Drive. She was close to some important homes: the Greenson house and that of Patricia (sister of JFK and Bobby) and her husband, the actor Peter Lawford, were a few minutes away, and Hanna Fenichel, the widow of the great psychoanalyst, lived just seventy metres from her door. Marilyn passed the last months of her life in this house under Eunice's "supervision". It was also the period in which a new psychoanalyst appeared on the scene to replace Greenson who left for Europe in May 1962. The new therapist was Milton

Wexler, a friend of Greenson's. He was another well-known Hollywood psychoanalyst who we will examine in the chapter on sexual relationships between analysts and their patients.

Marilyn's psychological state was undoubtedly deteriorating during the last weeks of her life. Her suicide by drug overdose fitted perfectly into her clinical history and her excessive reliance on pills. Eunice Murray explained the actress's death in terms of this dynamic both in her immediate statement to the police and in her memoirs published in 1975. According to Eunice, she awoke in a state of apprehension in the "early morning hours of 5 August, 1962". She was not woken by Marilyn's screams from yet another nightmare, but by an unusual silence. She found it strange that a telephone wire had been passed under the locked door of Marilyn's bedroom. Yet she couldn't hear anyone talking. It was about three in the morning and Eunice informed Greenson, who rushed down to his patient's home and broke the window of Marilyn's room in order to get in.

Marilyn was lying naked on the bed. She was not asleep but dead. She was holding the telephone in her right hand, and there was an empty bottle of Nembutal on the bedside table. The police were called at 4.25 in the morning on 5 August 1962. Jack Clemmons, the police sergeant who was the first to arrive on the scene after the "official" call, declared in 1967 that "it was the clearest case of murder I have ever seen". Suicide was the version that was immediately made public.

But that night at Marilyn's home was far from calm and strangely quiet. Gradually information began to come out from various sources, as Wolfe tells us in his meticulous biography. Marilyn died a few hours before she did in the official version, at around 10.45 p.m. on 4 August 1962. That night cars, unknown persons and policemen were coming and going. At some stage an ambulance arrived, although the time is disputed, and the neighbours clearly heard a helicopter. By the time the police were officially called at 4.25 a.m., all sorts of things had happened. Marilyn died in a room other than her bedroom, and only later was she carried to her bed.

Who was the last person to see Marilyn? Who did she telephone? What piece of news finally brought her down and drove her to suicide? It is well known that there are several theories concerning Marilyn's suicide: some perceived it as the predictable consequence of her psychological state and her family's psycho-pathological history, while others linked it to the fact that Robert Kennedy had ended their relationship. Equally there are many theories of a possible murder, which have been summarised by Farber and Green:

> [According to a first hypothesis] contained in a booklet for which Sergeant Clemmons supplied data and which was published two years after Marilyn's death, when Robert Kennedy was running for the U.S. Senate, the politically liberal Dr. Greenson was a fellow traveller who acted as the agent of a Communist Party plot to kill the actress because she threatened to expose her affair with Bobby Kennedy, the Reds' Manchurian candidate. According to an equally outlandish theory, Greenson was the agent of the Kennedys themselves, who wanted to silence Marilyn and save themselves from scandal. Still another alleges that she was killed by the CIA, which sought to discredit the Kennedys. In another, she was killed by the FBI, because J. Edgar Hoover wanted to seize her phone records and get the goods on Bobby. Yet another conjecture is that she was killed by the Mafia, to frame the Kennedys and drive them out of office. And one recent book even claims that Greenson himself had become so moonstruck

over Marilyn that he murdered his patient in a jealous rage.

Spoto puts forward yet another theory in his biography: Marilyn died from an overdose of Nembutal (according to the autopsy reports) contained in a suppository that Eunice Murray is supposed to have inserted in Marilyn's rectum on Greenson's instructions. According to Spoto, the Kennedys had nothing to do with Marilyn's death: Eunice and Greenson are supposed to have killed Marilyn out of an absurd resentment against the actress who wanted to dismiss them.

Lastly, Wolfe in the latest biography takes up the theory that Greenson was a Communist Party agent, which also involves Robert F. Kennedy in Marilyn's death. The book ends with a scene in which Greenson, Lawford and Bobby Kennedy escape in a Mercedes shortly after Marilyn's death. According to the biographer's final comment, "the evidence points to premeditated homicide. In the presence of Bobby Kennedy, she was injected with enough barbiturate to kill fifteen people."

What is clear is that everything revolved around Greenson. Disturbing information is provided by the opening and closing pages of the most recent biography of Marilyn: shortly after midnight on 4 August 1962 a black Mercedes was stopped for speeding by a policeman on Olympic Boulevard in Beverly Hills. When the officer looked into the car, he could not fail to recognise the United States Attorney General, Robert F. Kennedy, and his brother-in-law, the actor Peter Lawford, at the wheel. There was a third man, who was later identified as Dr. Greenson. Lawford said that he had to take the Attorney General urgently to the Beverly Hilton Hotel. Bobby's presence in Los Angeles was always denied after his name began to be connected with Marilyn's death. But in 1985, the housekeeper Eunice admitted that Bobby visited Marilyn on 4 August, and she was very definite in confirming that encounter: "Oh, sure, yes, I was in the living room when he arrived. She was not dressed." Bobby and Lawford went to Marilyn's between three and four in the afternoon and they left before 4.30. Eunice called Greenson, who arrived between four and five to calm the actress, who was suffering from a severe nervous crisis, and he stayed until seven. Robert Kennedy returned with two men between 9.30 and 10.00 in the evening. At 10.45 Marilyn was dying. A little before midnight, Ralph S. Greenson, Peter Lawford and Robert F. Kennedy were driving fast along an avenue in Beverly Hills.

Marilyn's death can be seen as the first in a chain of premature deaths affecting people who were close to her that day. Robert F. Kennedy was assassinated in 1968, Peter Lawford was destroyed by alcohol in 1972, and Greenson died in 1979 at sixty-eight, enfeebled both physically and psychologically. Although he was not present on that night, it is difficult to forget JFK, who died a year after Marilyn.

All examinations of Marilyn's death have ended up trying to understand the role of her psychoanalyst, Ralph S. Greenson. All the biographers agree that Greenson knew what really happened on the evening of 4 August 1962. When books and newspapers started to mention his name – often disparagingly as in Spoto's biography – Greenson and his family undertook various lawsuits to protect his good name and professional honour. But these proved to be useless: Greenson was pestered incessantly by journalists and photographers from immediately after Marilyn's death, every time an article, interview or book came out in which his name was mentioned. Greenson, who was very distressed by Marilyn's death, went to New York to see Max Schur, who had been Sigmund Freud's doctor. He needed a series of sessions to confront and overcome his psychological difficulties. He began to miss appointments with his patients. He was absent-minded and depressed, and he cried during sessions. Study was a comfort, and Greenson devoted his energies to writing a massive treatise on psychoanalytical technique. His penchant for expressing strong opinions was briefly reawakened in 1973, when *The Exorcist* was released and he wrote a strongly worded article criticizing the way in which the psychiatric profession was presented in the film. "*The Exorcist* is a menace to our community. It should be X-rated," Greenson wrote in a high-circulation weekly (*Saturday Review/World*, 1974).

The last years of his life were marked by depression, repeated cardiovascular disorders, and finally episodes of aphasia ("That was very hard for someone who had so many words for everything," as the actress Janice Rule observed, having been another of his patients). The legal disputes over his involvement in Marilyn's death continued even after his death in 1979. The Swiss weekly magazine *Blick*, which in 1985 published material considered defamatory to Greenson's memory, was ordered to pay damages, and part of the money went to the Anna Freud Centre in London.

There were suspicions that Greenson had other interests in the actress: something that went beyond counter-transference under analysis or even a sexual relationship as some colleagues suggested. Wolfe's biography provides new details. In short, Greenson is supposed to have been in the American Communist Party and to have hosted cell meetings in Hollywood. The charge is that he was engaged in obtaining the maximum amount of information on American government politics by word of mouth through Marilyn, who supposedly received such information from JFK and more especially from Bobby, and noted it down in a famous diary that disappeared at the time of her death. Wolfe produces CIA documents that prove that Marilyn was under surveillance for her unwitting position as a go-between for Soviet agents and important figures in American politics during the Cold War. An FBI document, which alarmed its director J. Edgar Hoover, referred to a meeting in Mexico City between Marilyn and Frederick Vanderbilt Field, one of the best-known exponents of the American Communist Party. The latter had been director of the American-Russian Institute, on whose executive committee Greenson's mother had sat. During the anti-communist campaign of the fifties, Field moved to Mexico City with some of his comrades. These included Churchill Murray, the brother-in-law of Eunice, Marilyn's housekeeper. Eunice's husband John was also a member of the Communist Party, as was Marilyn's doctor, Hyman Engelberg. Greenson's links with this group will only be understood when we are able to consult his FBI file, which is still considered a state secret for reasons of "internal security". However, the personal accounts gathered by Wolfe appear to demonstrate that Greenson was responsible for maintaining contacts between Field in Mexico and his comrades in the United States.

According to Wolfe, Greenson's commitment to the communist cause can be explained by his cultural and ideological roots, which went back to the foundation of the Institute of Psychoanalysis in Berlin and a group of psychoanalysts who attempted to combine psycho-analysis with Marxism. Freudian-Marxism was closely linked to the political struggle, and many of these psychoanalysts were members of the Communist Party or the Socialist Party. They argued that psychoanalysis should not be a privilege of the wealthy bourgeoisie, and should be extended to the proletariat. The Institute's founding members included Ernst Simmel and Otto Fenichel, who moved to Los Angeles in 1934 and 1938 respectively. Simmel, who had been one of Sigmund Freud's students and worked very closely with him, became one of Hollywood's best known psychoanalysts. His patients included the scriptwriter Herman Mankiewicz (who co-scripted *Citizen Kane* with Orson Welles) and the musician George Gershwin. Kris and Rudolph Loewenstein had also studied at the Berlin Institute and later they both became analysts in New York (as we have already seen, the former was Marilyn's analyst as well as Jacqueline Kennedy's; the latter was the analyst of Arthur Miller, Marilyn's third husband). A group was formed around Simmel to discuss politics, art, literature and cinema. These Californian encounters were frequented by leading intellectuals (such as Theodor W. Adorno, Bertolt Brecht, Max Horkheimer, Fritz Lang and Thomas Mann), as well as several psychoanalysts such as Fenichel and Greenson. Of course many of the intellectuals were under surveillance by the FBI and some of them were accused of anti-American activities. Hollywood's communist wing was linked into the Arts, Sciences and Professions Council, as well as the party organisation which is alleged to have met secretly at the home of Murray or Greenson.

Marilyn could not have had the slightest idea about her Jesus's cultural and political background. However, if we were to give credence to Greenson's direct or indirect involvement as a Soviet informer, we would first need to explain the many aspects of the Monroe affair that appear to suggest no overriding desire to keep the actress alive in order to gather information. Why did Greenson prescribe her such heavy doses of drugs? Why, when he was injecting Marilyn with adrenaline in an attempt to revive her, did he insert the needle so badly that, if we are to believe one of Wolfe's witnesses, he undid the beneficial effect the injection was supposed to have? What about the claim that he was seen in a black Mercedes with Bobby Kennedy and Peter Lawford around midnight? In other words, why would he have wanted Marilyn's death if he was interested in state secrets that he could only obtain if she remained alive? According to Wolfe, Marilyn's death was in the end a relief for everyone: for the Kennedys, who had been freed from the nightmare of a scandal; for the CIA and the FBI, who were reassured about a possible leak of secret material; and for Greenson, who had been released from a personal and professional commitment that was becoming too demanding.

In his treatise on *The Technique and Practice of Psychoanalysis*, Greenson writes at length on the relationship between the analyst and the patient, and the problems of transference and countertransference. He argues that

> ... one cannot work analytically unless one can oscillate between the relatively detached analytic position and the more involved physicianly one. The analyst must be a person who can empathise and feel compassion sincerely and yet use restraint.

Many colleagues felt that Greenson's interest in Marilyn was, at the very least, excessive. It was pointed out that, even in the case of family therapy, it was never considered normal practice to take a patient home, constantly invite her to lunch and make her a friend of one's wife and children. Malicious tongues suggested that four or five hours in the company of the most seductive woman in America couldn't fail to win the heart of the Romeo of psychoanalysis in California. While Marilyn was still alive, Greenson argued that analysis would be more effective if she were shown the model of a family and the emotional context that she lacked in childhood. After her death, the critical voices could not be silenced. Greenson gave the following justification of the type of therapy he used for Marilyn in a 1973 issue of the *Medical Tribune*:

> It is controversial, I know that. Nevertheless, I have practised for some thirty-five years, and I did what I thought best, particularly after other methods of treatment apparently hadn't touched her one iota... I did it for a purpose. My particular method of treatment for this particular woman was, I thought, essential at that time. But it failed. She died.

On at least two other occasions, Greenson referred to some aspects of the Monroe affair: in his essay on *Transitional Objects and Transference* and his unpublished work *Special Problems in Psychotherapy with the Rich and Famous*. Even though he did not refer to the case of Norma J. or Marilyn M., the details clearly point to the famous actress. Greenson was certainly tormented by the question of Marilyn's transference or dependency. But he did nothing to stem this emotional tie. When he went to a conference in Europe in May 1962, the role of substitute analyst was entrusted to a chess piece, as is made clear in "Transitional Objects and Transference":

> The young woman had recently been given a gift of a carved iron chess set... As she looked at the set through the sparkling light of a glass of champagne, it suddenly struck her that I looked like the white knight of her chess set. The realisation evoked in her

a feeling of comfort... The white knight was a protector, it belonged to her, she could carry it wherever she went, it would look after her, and I could go on my merry way to Europe without having to worry about her.

Marilyn was worried about the public appearance she was to make in Madison Square Garden in New York for JFK's birthday celebrations. But as a transitional object in psychoanalytical terms (like Linus's blanket), the white knight would protect her. On 19 May 1962, Marilyn famously sang "Happy birthday to you" to the President of the United States and thousands of spectators. Greenson wrote in his paper:

> The patient's major concern about the period of my absence was a public performance of great importance to her. She now felt confident of success because she could conceal her white knight in her handkerchief or scarf; she was certain that he would protect her from nervousness, anxiety, or bad luck. I was relieved and delighted to learn, while in Europe, that her performance had been a smashing success.

Following a party in the penthouse of the theatrical impresario Arthur Krim, Marilyn and JFK took a complex route which Wolfe describes in detail. It involved taking lifts and walking along basements to avoid journalists in order to reach the President's penthouse which enjoyed a spectacular view of Manhattan. It was the last time that Marilyn and JFK saw each other, sixteen years after they first met and three months before her death. In a letter of 20 January 1963 to Greenson, Anna Freud expressed the following feelings about Marilyn's death:

> I am terribly sorry about Marilyn Monroe. I know exactly how you feel because I had exactly the same

thing happen with a patient of mine who took cyanide two days before I came back from America a few years ago. One goes over and over in one's head to find out where one could have done better and it leaves one with a terrible sense of being defeated. But, you know, I think in these cases we are really defeated by something which is stronger than we are and for which analysis, with all its powers, is too weak a weapon.

Anna Freud perhaps did not realise that the case of Marilyn Monroe was much more complicated. It was not simply a matter of a difficult analysis and the suicide of another patient. The case of Marilyn Monroe was exemplary, primarily because it brought together many aspects of the historical development of psychoanalysis (which began to spread after the treatment of some famous cases, such as Anna O. and Emmy von N.), but also because it highlighted many critical and controversial aspects of psychoanalytical therapy that will be discussed in later chapters.

In the first place, relationships between patients and analysts do not only entangle these two persons, occasionally leading into sexual relationships (see Chapter 3), but also involve other people (relations, friends and other psychoanalysts) who are linked into a "constellation" of emotional ties and interests.

The Marilyn M. constellation is a complex network of people and relationships (Fig. 2). Without going into all the possible links, the following are sufficient to give an idea of their intricacy. Marilyn was analysed by Marianne Rie Kris, who in turn was analysed by Anna Freud, and Anna Freud also analysed Marilyn. Anna had been analysed by her father Sigmund, who had

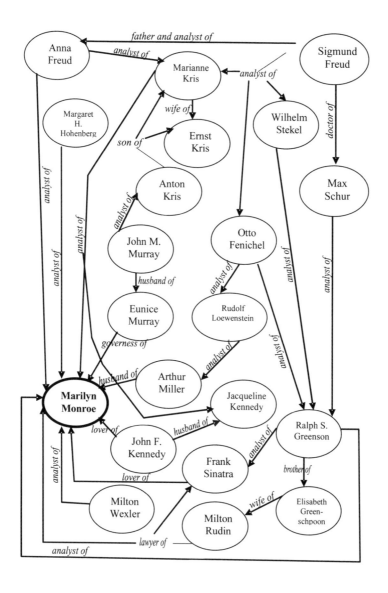

Fig. 2. The constellation for Marilyn Monroe

also analysed Marianne Kris, as well as Otto Fenichel and Wilhelm Stekel. Otto Fenichel was later to be the analyst of Rudolph Loewenstein and Ralph Greenson, who had also been analysed by Stekel. Marilyn married Arthur Miller, who was analysed by Loewenstein, and had a relationship with Frank Sinatra, who was analysed by Greenson. The relationship with John F. Kennedy leads back to Marianne Rie Kris, one of whose patients was Jacqueline, the President's wife. Moroever, Marilyn's housekeeper had, according to Wolfe, been married to John M. Murray, who had analysed Anton Kris, the son of Marianne Rie and Ernst Kris (here you could start to go into the network around Marianne Kris illustrated in Fig. 1). Apart from the love affairs, we can examine the professional relationships in the network: Elizabeth Greenschpoon, the psychoanalyst's sister, married Milton Rudin, and Milton was the lawyer and agent of both Sinatra and Marilyn, i.e. two patients of his brother-in-law Ralph Greenson, and two patients linked by a sexual relationship.

The constellation is something more than the sum of its parts: it is a *Gestalt*, a form or structure that is refashioned every time a new element is added. Marilyn was drawn into this web: she was treated in London by Anna Freud, who was a childhood friend of her psychoanalyst Marianne Rie Kris, who, in turn, had a son in analysis with the husband of Marilyn's housekeeper. Marilyn was having a sexual relationship with Sinatra, who was being analysed by her own analyst and whose business affairs were being dealt with by her analyst's brother-in-law, and so it went on.

The emotions and information that passed along the threads of this web formed the setting in which Marilyn's psychological life was played out, as with the other characters in the plot. A constellation could be drawn around any one of these characters, as has already been done for Rie Kris (Fig. 1) and Marilyn (Fig. 2). But it is not only a useful abstraction and a means of interpreting each of their lives. In reality, the network or constellation is the dominant force. It is an "analytical cyberspace" and a "collective emotional intelligence" that governs the lives of members from above. However, the constellation can be adjusted or reorganised from below, if one of its elements crosses a certain threshold and puts the system in jeopardy. Hence Marilyn's death, the product of this web, altered its entire system and shook the constellations formed around the other characters.

If you look at the photo taken on the yacht *Manitou* four days after the actress's funeral, you will see a group made up of President JFK, his sister Patricia (a great friend of Marilyn's), his brother-in-law Peter Lawford, and Pat Newcomb (who looked after Marilyn's public relations, and had been with Marilyn on the afternoon of 4 August, shortly before her death, and became inconsolable later when she saw her corpse). Looking at that row of smiling sets of white teeth as they pose with the stars and stripes flapping in the wind, it can be clearly understood how the constellations of each one were shifting with Marilyn's passing. Similarly, if you look at Greenson's face during her funeral and think about his subsequent depression, it is equally clear how Marilyn's death had changed his network, albeit in a different way.

The case of Marilyn M. provides an extreme example of another important aspect of psychoanalytical treatment. Each case is not just a history, but a history of histories, a spiral of interpretations and reassessments. Of one thing we can be certain, it will continue to be necessary to go back over the case of Marilyn M. New information will challenge previous interpretations. There will never be any certainty. A case is a reconstruction of events and their interpretation. It is not an objective and verifiable fact. It is instead the product of a continuous reshuffling of information, omissions and half-truths. In the end, it becomes a story that gradually transforms and modifies itself as it is narrated and handed down. A clinical case in psychoanalysis is therefore not just a fiction in itself. Everything that happens around the case also becomes a fiction. An analyst's life cannot be detached from the cases he or she treats, because they are structurally interwoven. The public facts differ from what is known privately. Then private facts are released and the public and private versions blend into a new all-embracing fictionalised version.

In the end, no one can really know what happened. But then psychoanalysis does not go in search of the truth. It is interested in an interpretation, a plausible account of how things *might* have gone, but also an account that has the fascination of a crime-thriller.

Chapter 2
Analysts' children

Psychologists have always paid particular attention to their own children. Some children have made their parents famous by being the source of their psychological theories. Jean Piaget systematically observed the sensory, motor and cognitive development of his three children (and used the information acquired to produce his great work *The Origins of Intelligence in Children*), Lev S. Vygotsky studied the mental processes of his two sons at length, and Burrhus F. Skinner kept his daughter in a very special cot (of the so-called "Skinner box" type that he had designed for his experiments on rats), which contained ropes, levers and instruments to record the simpler forms of learning during the early months of life. A great deal is known about the early babbling and the first words of the writer Günther Anders, because they were recorded in the books of his parents, the psychologists Clara and William Stern.

Psychoanalysts went even further with their children. Not only did they study them, they also treated them in the analytical sense, in some cases from when they were very small. Clearly there is an added complication when the observation of one's own children is psychological in general, but more especially when it is psychoanalytical. Because psychoanalysis considers the relationship between parents and children central to an understanding of an individual's psychological development, this relationship is affected if one or both of the parents do not experience that relationship in a completely natural manner, but always reflect it through the mirror of analysis. Every act, every word and every gesture is constantly interpreted through this particular approach, and one's behaviour towards one's child is modified in relation to this interpretation. Any "naturalness" in interpersonal relations is lost. When actual analysis is involved, the situation becomes even more complicated. According to the fundamental mechanism of transference, a process identified by psychoanalysis, one of the patient's two parent figures is identified in the analyst. In this case, however, the distinction between the identified figure and the real figure is almost reduced to nothing. The parent figure is identified with the parent.

This paradoxical situation was initiated by none other than Sigmund Freud, who started to analyse his daughter Anna in 1918 and continued for a total of four years. This error by the founding father of psychoanalysis was so serious that it was never made public by anyone who knew about it (such as Ernest Jones, Sigmund Freud's "official" biographer). Many psychoanalysts believed that Anna's analysis was carried out by Lou Andreas-Salomé and when Paul Roazen revealed the truth in 1969 in his book on the psychoanalyst Viktor Tausk, they continued to deny it. No, it wasn't possible. Anna analysed by her father, whatever next! At the same time, psychoanalysts used one of their favourite defence mechanisms and argued that this point had been known about for some time and was therefore hardly worth discussing. In more recent works, Roazen has quite rightly stressed that until he revealed the, to say the very least, complicated analytical situation between father and daughter, no one had made the slightest reference to it in writing.

In 1970 Edoardo Weiss, the well known Italian psychoanalyst who emigrated to the United States in

1939 because of the race laws, published a book of personal accounts and a series of letters received from Sigmund Freud. In one letter dated 10 November 1935, Freud responded to Weiss's question about the possibility of a son being analysed by his father by saying that he "succeeded well" with Anna, but "there are special difficulties and doubts with a son". These words were a direct confirmation that Freud had analysed his daughter. Anna was not at all pleased with Roazen's historical discovery and claimed: "He is busy trying to dig up whatever negative facts about personalities he can. This includes my father and me and what he cannot find he invents." Equally she considered Weiss's book to be "ambivalent, ungrateful and somehow mean."

Besides, Anna followed her father's example, and he in turn had been influenced by contemporary psychologists. Just as Freud filled his books with his own fantasies and dreams, and those of his children, Anna in her first published work as an analyst, *Beating Fantasies and Daydreams* (1922), spoke of a case that is believed to have been her personal experience. In fact it appears to be the same case of "psychasthenia" that was described by Sigmund in his essay *A Child is Being Beaten* (1919). In her article, Anna described the three stages of fantasy: "The first was the creation of the beating fantasy, which was itself a substitute for an incestuous father-daughter love scene that was distorted by repression, and regression to the anal-sadistic phase finds expression as a beating scene, the climax of which coincided with masturbatory gratification" (Young-Bruehl). Subsequently, this was followed by a phase of "nice stories" and "fantasised beautiful scenes", often themselves followed by masturbation.

This was the period in which Anna started to write poetry and short pieces of prose with explicit reference to her fantasies filled with scenes of violence and to the sin of masturbation. Her poem *Night* ends with a few lines addressed to an unknown person who, in the opinion of Young-Bruehl, is perhaps the person who prohibited the "sin":

> Why are you happy, when I toss in my bed,
> When I stretch my arms wide but let them
> Fall empty on my body. Close the door!

In the poem *Dreams*, Anna describes herself in the following terms:

> And so I am thinking: in your life
> You would have found several loves,
> Only clear sight was not given you,
> Your heart stood open to other thoughts.
> Tighter than the shoes upon your feet,
> Fears, obsessions, obstinacy gripped
> Your mind; affectless, repulsed by things,
> You turned your longing in on yourself.

Regard for Anna, the master's daughter, grew mostly after his death in 1939. She had the task of handing down and spreading psychoanalysis in its most orthodox version, the one most faithful to her father's thought. In this, Anna was not a lone heroic voice, just as Sigmund had not been a lone heroic voice when he conceived his theory. Anna lived within a kind of extended family. The love that this family provided was a great support through her private and professional vicissitudes, particularly after her move to London.

The Freud family, once the sons had left, was made up of Sigmund, his wife Martha, Martha's sister Minna Bernays, Anna and from 1929 the housekeeper Paula Fichtl. It then extended to another family, that of

Dorothy Burlingham, who in Vienna used to live in the flat above the Freuds (the two flats were linked by an internal telephone line). The relationship with Dorothy was a fundamental part of Anna's life, but it was also another typical analytical constellation. Daughter of Louis Comfort Tiffany, the great glass-maker, Dorothy married Robert Burlingham, who also belonged to one of New York's very rich families. Robert, a surgeon, was seriously psychotic, and Dorothy left him and went to Vienna to treat the psychological problems of her ten-year-old son Robert (Bob), who suffered from asthma. Anna first analysed Bob and then his siblings, Marv (Mabbie), Katrina (Tinky) and Michael (Mikey). Initially Dorothy and her children shared a flat with the Sweetzers, an American family (little Adelaide and Harold Sweetzer were also under analysis with Anna). For her part, Dorothy started analysis with Theodor Reik, and later had another treatment with Sigmund Freud. To use Dorothy's own words, the friendship with Anna was "the most precious relationship" that she had ever had, and Anna's father was delighted about it, as he wrote to Binswanger in 1929: "Our symbiosis with an American family (husbandless), whose children my daughter is bringing up analytically with a firm hand, is growing continually stronger, so that we share with them our needs for the summer."

That wonderful period before her departure from Vienna for London has been described very well by Anna's biographer, Young-Bruehl:

> The Burlinghams moved into the apartment above the Freuds'; they had summer houses next door to the Freuds' summer houses; Dorothy transported everyone in her automobile; the children played with the Freud grandchildren, especially Ernst Halberstadt, who spent much of his adolescence with the Freuds and became Bob Burlingham's best friend.

Starting in 1927, Dorothy Burlingham and Anna Freud took vacation trips together, leaving their families to keep each other company; and in 1930 they bought a cottage in the Semmering together so that any of the families' members who wished could join in for country weekends. This cottage, named Hochroterd (High Red Earth), was the physical place where there was no need to keep a distance in order to be at home.

Inevitably, the relationship between Anna and Dorothy was eventually considered to be homosexual. It appears that only the loyal housekeeper Paula Fichtl did not realise it. The journalist Detlef Berthelsen pointed out in his book based on Paula's memories: "The significance of the relationship between Dorothy Burlingham and Anna Freud also escaped Paula. Even in her old age, the word 'lesbian' meant nothing to her. However, when Dorothy Burlingham telephoned, she felt jealous."

The question is not so much Anna's homosexuality as the intrigue that it set in motion, which has been traced by Berthelsen: Dorothy Burlingham's children "were analysed by Anna Freud, who was after all their mother's lover, and their mother had been analysed by Anna's father, who previously had probed his daugher's psyche."

Her biographer Young-Bruehl argues that the relationship was platonic:

> After her fashion, she [Anna] had a rich and full family life, though she did not, in the 1920s or afterwards, have a sexual relationship, with Dorothy Burlingham or with anyone else. She remained a "vestal" – to use the apt word Marie Bonaparte later chose to signal both Anna Freud's virginity and her role as the chief keeper of her father's person and his science, psychoanalysis.

Others, like Berthelsen, believed that it was a practising homosexual relationship, and that homosexuality became one of the distinctive features of female psychoanalysts who worked at the Hampstead clinic founded by Anna: "Those women", she wrote, "had to meet at least two of three essential conditions: they had to be very intelligent, Jewish and lesbian".

Anna treated homosexuality with caution, and she did not feel it appropriate to consider it normal or natural behaviour, unlike her father who had spoken of it as "nothing to be ashamed of, no vice, no degradation, it cannot be classified as an illness", but should be considered "a variation of the sexual function produced by a certain arrest of sexual development" (*Letters*, 9 April 1935).

The Burlingham component of Freud's extended family did not have a happy time. In 1938 Robert, Dorothy's husband, killed himself by jumping from the fourteenth floor of a skyscraper. Although he suffered from serious mental disorders, he had always been sceptical and hostile towards psychoanalysis. His father, an eminent lawyer, took legal action to remove his grandchildren from Dorothy and the Freuds, whom he considered deviants as far as the children's education was concerned. Even those who trusted in psychoanalysis did not meet a pleasant end. Bob, the first of the children to undergo analysis with Anna (and later with the Freud's loyal follower Kurt Eissler), died of a heart attack in 1970 at the age of fifty-four, after constant manic episodes, depression and physical self-neglect had reduced him to a skeleton (Bob suffered from asthma, but smoked excessively). However, there is another version of Bob's death, which is told by the journalist Berthelsen, although she mistakes his name for that of his brother Michael:

> During the seventies, a tragedy occurred at Maresfield Gardens that has been a carefully held secret. [Bob], the eldest of Dorothy's children, came to visit them. He was fifty years old and irreparably stricken by tuberculosis, which he inherited from his mother. One Sunday, while his mother and Anna Freud were at Walberswick [where Anna and Dorothy had a house for weekends and holidays], he swallowed a fatal dose of sleeping pills and lay down on Anna Freud's psychiatric couch, which he knew from his childhood. That is where the two women found him, already a corpse, when they returned home the following morning.... The funeral took place in the utmost secrecy.

Dorothy's daughter Mabbie developed a profound dependence in relation to her past analyst. When she was undergoing analysis with Marianne Rie Kris in New York (Kris had also been the analyst of Bob's wife Rigmor Sorensen, who was nicknamed Mossik), she constantly referred to Anna. She suffered from depression. In 1974 she visited her mother and Anna in London, took an overdose of sleeping pills and died in their house. Rather surprisingly the tragic deaths of two of Dorothy's children, who were amongst the very first to be treated with child psychoanalysis by, what is more, one of its leading exponents and perhaps the best known, is not given the prominence in the history of psychoanalysis that it undoubtedly merits. The dramatic outcome of the analysis of these two people has not been of much concern to Anna Freud's biographers and historians of psychoanalysis. Yet Anna loved them so much that she wrote at the beginning of the analysis in 1926 to Max Eitingon, one of the first members of the Freudian circle:

> I think sometimes that I want not only to make them healthy but also, at the same time, to have them, or at least have something of them, for myself. Temporarily, of course, this desire is useful for my work, but sometime or another it really will disturb them, and so, on the whole, I really cannot call my need other than stupid.

After these deaths, relations between the children of Bob and Mabbie and their grandmother Dorothy and her friend Anna became cool, as can be seen from the unflattering biography that Bob's son, Michael John, wrote of his grandmother. Michael bitterly declared: "There remains the ironic conclusion that psychoanalysis had been foisted upon them unnecessarily, and when dependent upon it, had not helped them. Then, when they had really needed help, Freudian ideology had discouraged them from seeking it, for example, in the realm of pharmacology."

Anna Freud also analysed Ernst Simmel's son Reinhard in 1927, while Ernst Simmel was analysed by Karl Abraham, who had also been a member of the select group of Freud's original disciples. Reinhard had also been analysed by Melanie Klein, who was the other authority along with Anna on child psychoanalysis between the wars.

Melanie also started with her own children. Her first contribution to child psychoanalysis (*The Development of a Child*, 1921) concerned the case of little Fritz, who was in fact her son Erich. Melanie had intentionally hidden the identity of her young "subject", as she explained in her letter of 14 December 1920 to Sándor Ferenczi, another leading psychoanalyst:

> As I told you, with regard to the more intimate details I think it necessary to conceal that the subject of the second study is my son. This will,

however, sever the connection with the first study, which is perhaps a shame.... I would like to change my son Erich into little Fritz, the son of relations of mine, whose mother had been faithfully following my instructions and whom I had often the opportunity to see informally. If the change from 'Erich' to 'Fritz', and from 'I' to 'the mother' is applied throughout the study, I think the disguise will be perfect.

And so it happened. In 1921 the article appeared in German in the magazine *Imago* (and then in English in 1923 in *International Journal of Psychoanalysis*). This is how Klein wrote about the "case" of a child with whom she had had the "occasion to be much occupied":

The child in question is a boy, little Fritz, the son of relations who live in my immediate neighbourhood. This gave me the opportunity to be often in the child's company without any restraint. Further, as his mother follows all my recommendations I am able to exercise a far-reaching influence on the child's upbringing.

Melanie could quite easily have explained the case and the analysis she provided without saying that the child in question was her son. She would have been acting like doctors or psychologists who for reasons of confidentiality restrict themselves to referring to the patients by their initials. There was no need for her to say that he was "the son of relations", who lived in the "immediate neighbourhood" and the mother followed her "recommendations". In this way, readers are led into an unreal and fictional dimension, in which they imagine Klein going to visit the family, meeting close to her home, and so on. Did she really need to engage in fictional narration and construct such a complex edifice? Not only did Klein use the story of her own child and interpret it in accordance with her theoretical model, but she also inserted it within another story, that of Klein and her involvement in the lives of Fritz and his mother.

It is a strange mother, who asks her son about his ideas on methods of mating for the purposes of conception. Fritz thought that children were made from milk, but his mother put him right using the educative principles of psychoanalysis. We do not know exactly how old he was when this didactic conversation took place, but Fritz was certainly younger than six:

(Mother) "Real children are not made of food."

He, "I know that, they are made of milk."

"Oh, no, they are made of something that papa makes and the egg that is inside mamma." (He is very attentive now and asks me to explain.)

When I begin once more about the little egg, he interrupts me, "I know that."

I continue, "Papa can make something with his wiwi that really looks rather like milk and is called seed; he makes it like doing wiwi only not so much. Mamma's wiwi is different to papa's."

(He interrupts) "I know *that*!"

I say, "Mamma's wiwi is like a hole. If papa puts his wiwi into mamma's wiwi and makes the seed there, then the seed runs in deeper into her body and when it meets with one of the little eggs that are inside mamma, then the little egg begins to grow and it becomes a child."

Fritz listens with great interest and says, "I would so much like to see how a child is made inside like that." I explain that this is impossible until he is big because it can't be done till then but that he will do it himself. "But then I would like to do it to mamma."

The mother, who fortunately always follows Klein's advice, does not bat an eyelid and replies to the little boy:

> That can't be, mamma can't be your wife for she is the wife of your papa, and then papa would have no wife.

Then Fritz proves to be rather sharp, in spite of having been introduced as a child with a "slow mental development" and incapable of "especially remarkable sayings, such as one hears at a very early age sometimes from gifted children." He promptly retorts: "But we could both do it to her." To which the mother concludes:

> No, that can't be. Every man has only one wife. When you are big your mamma will be old. Then you will marry a beautiful young girl and she will be your wife.

Then there are the conversations that are not didactic but interpretative in relation to Fritz's thoughts. For example, Fritz has a particular fantasy about the stomach and the belly, and mummy kindly provides him with an immediate interpretation.

> "There is a room in the stomach, in it there are tables and chairs. Someone sits down on a chair and lays his head on the table and then the whole house falls down, the ceiling on the floor, the table too tumbles down, the house tumbles down." To my question, "Who is someone and how did he get inside?" he answers, "A little stick came through the wiwi into the belly and into the stomach that way." In this instance he offered little resistance to my interpretation.

Little resistance: perhaps Fritz had had enough of mummy's interpretations.

I told him that he had imagined himself in his mamma's place and wished his papa might do with him what he does with her. But he is afraid (as he imagines his mamma to be too) that if this stick - papa's wiwi – gets into his wiwi he will be hurt and then inside his belly, in his stomach, everything will be destroyed, too.

Before his analysis, Fritz was frightened of Grimm's Fairy Tales, but afterwards – as Klein proudly observed – they became his favourites. It would not be surprising if Erich felt that things could hardly get worse. Those fairy stories must have seemed really tame after mummy's stories about a stick that he wanted to have stuck in his tummy, if only it did not hurt him! But this was the price to be paid for normal psychological development:

> We shall let the child acquire as much sexual information as the growth of its desire for knowledge requires, thus depriving sexuality at once of its mystery and of a great part of its danger. This ensures that wishes, thoughts and feelings shall not – as happened to us – be partly repressed and partly, in so far as repression fails, endured under a burden of false shame and nervous suffering. In averting this repression, this burden of superfluous suffering, moreover, we are laying the foundation for health, mental balance and the favourable development of character.

Melanie adopted the same approach when she analysed her other children, Hans and Melitta. While Erich had been called Fritz (and possibly also Ernst in another publication), Hans was disguised as Felix, and Melitta as Grete (and perhaps as Lisa in another work). However Melanie's analysis proved insufficient for the children.

Erich was also analysed by Clara Happel (who had been analysed by Hanns Sachs), Nina Searl (one of Melanie's faithful disciples), Donald W. Winnicott (who had been analysed by James Strachey; his wife Clare Winnicott was analysed by Melanie) and Betty Joseph (who had been analysed by Paula Heimann, who in turn had been analysed by Melanie).

Hans was analysed by Ernst Simmel (who had been analysed by Karl Abraham).

Melitta was analysed by Max Eitingon (who had been analysed by Sigmund Freud), Karen Horney (who had been analysed by Karl Abraham and Hanns Sachs), Ella Sharpe (who had been analysed by James Glover, brother of Edward Glover; James had also been Alix Strachey's analyst) and Edward Glover (who had been analysed by Karl Abraham).

Klein wrote about the three children in various articles in the early twenties, in which she dwelt upon their sexual fantasies and their interpretations. Here is an example of an instant interpretation of one of Hans's fantasies:

> The idea that occurred to him once in school was that the master, who, standing in front of the pupils, had leant his back against the desk, should fall down, knock over the desk, break it and hurt himself in so doing, demonstrated the significance of the teacher as father, and of the desk as mother, and this led to his sadistic conception of coitus.

What would Hans, who "had a general dislike for school", have had to conjure up if he had wanted to fantasise about his professor really hurting himself? Hans, ironically called Felix, met a tragic end. He underwent "370 hours" of analysis over "three and a quarter years" and, like Fritz, he was "of course" not Klein's son: "When the thirteen-year-old Felix was brought to me for analysis, he illustrated strikingly what Alexander has termed the 'neurotic character'." Given that "his mother" had told Klein that "for some months he had had a tic", Melanie concentrated her attention on the origins of Felix's tic, and devoted an article to this specific question in 1925 (*A Contribution to the Psychogenesis of Tics*). Felix, who had a passion for masturbation, used to meet up with a friend for "a mutual masturbation session". His father, who constantly kept an eye on his behaviour, used to hit him, while his mother Melanie, in her role as analyst, subjected him to interpretations of his fantasies during masturbation.

Hans loved music, and his mother believed that this passion was being inhibited once he started masturbating and would reappear if he desisted from the practice. When Hans moved on to a heterosexual relationship, it was incumbent upon the analyst-mother to take action:

> Felix's first heterosexual object choice was much influenced by his homosexual attitude. For him this actress [with whom he had a relationship] possessed male attributes, she was the mother with a penis. This attitude persisted in his relation to his second heterosexual love object. He fell in love with a girl who was older than himself and had taken the initiative in the matter. She personified his early childhood picture of his mother as a prostitute, at the same time also that of the mother with a penis who was superior to him. The transference proved strong enough for me to impose a temporary break in this relationship, particularly since Felix had already reached the insight that feelings of anxiety were bound up with these relationships.

Hans died in 1934, at the age of twenty-seven. During a trip to the mountains, he fell off a cliff. His sister Melitta believed that it was suicide, an opinion shared by some English psychoanalysts.

Melitta's relationship with her mother was more complex and tortured. She too, under the guise of Grete and Lisa in Klein's accounts, was subjected to analysis in which the interpretation of episodes and fantasies in sexual terms was fundamental:

> Grete sang first voice in the school choir; the schoolmistress came quite close to her seat and looked straight into her mouth. At this Grete felt an irresistible need to hug and kiss the teacher. In this analysis the girl's stammering proved to be determined by the libidinal cathexis of speaking as well as of singing. The rise and fall of the voice and the movements of the tongue represented coitus.

In 1934, at the age of thirty, Melitta declared her independence from her mother. She had graduated in medicine and was herself to become a psychoanalyst. She asserted in a letter sent that year:

> I must be allowed to have interests, friends, feelings and thoughts which are different or even contrary to yours. I do not think that an adult woman's relationship with her mother, however good, should be the centre of her life. I hope you do not expect from my analysis that I shall again take an attitude towards you which is similar to the one I had until a few years ago. This was one of neurotic dependence.

Melitta undertook further analysis with Edward Glover, under whom she formed a morbid, bitter and hateful attitude towards Melanie (Melitta wrote in 1971: "Edward Glover and I had agreed to ally to fight"). Melitta and Edward never failed to attack Melanie in meetings of the British Society of Psychoanalysis. Melitta accused her mother of taking away her clients, and analysing very small children –

an accusation to which the mother responded by claiming to never go under two and a half years. Edward was no less forthright, and unleashed an extremely bitter defamatory campaign against Melanie, who in his opinion was guilty of having caused a dangerous schism from genuine Freudian psychoanalytical theory. Edward and Melitta developed a kind of *folie à deux.* Glover was not supposed to have established a romantic liaison with Melitta – as some had thought, giving credence to the story that they had been seen holding hands at some international conference – but rather to have found in Melitta a substitute for his daughter who suffered from Down's syndrome.

In 1924, Melitta had married Walter Schmideberg, the educated and sophisticated son of a rich shipowner. After having met Max Eitingon, Sigmund Freud and Sándor Ferenczi, and having subscribed to psychoanalysis, Walter contributed to the foundation of the Psychoanalytical Polyclinic in Berlin. For a long time, Walter was a frequent visitor to Sigmund Freud's home in Vienna and he helped the family out with food and provisions during the difficult period of the First World War. In London too, he and Melitta would often visit the Freuds (including Anna, her mother's rival).

Walter was an alcoholic, a drug-user and a homosexual. In the mid-thirties he started a relationship with the writer Winifred Ellerman, whose pseudonym was Bryher. Winifred had a relationship with the well-known American poet Hilda Doolittle, who was also bisexual (she was the wife of the writer Richard Aldington) and often used other names: either the man's name John Helfort or the initials H.D. Hilda had been analysed by Sigmund Freud in Vienna (an experience she recounted in a book) and later by Walter himself.

At the end of the Second World War, Winifred and Walter moved to Switzerland and took Hilda's daughter, Perdita Schaffner, into their home. Melitta continued to have good relations with Walter (she went to see him and his partner Winifred in their Swiss home). Melanie's biographer, Phyllis S. Grosskurth, has commented: "No one has been able to understand this strange three-sided relationship." Walter died in 1954 from an ulcer caused by alcoholism. In the meantime Melitta had moved to New York, where she devoted herself to destitute and delinquent children, and eventually abandoned psychoanalysis. For years she had not been speaking to her mother. When Melanie died in September 1960, Melitta, who was also in London, did not go to her funeral. Melanie's biographer noted: "Melitta, unreconciled to the end, gave a lecture in London that day, wearing flamboyant red boots." Melanie remembered her daughter in her will, leaving her some jewellery of consequence, but added a final rather superfluous thought:

> My gold flexible bracelet which was given to me by my late husband, my gold necklace with garnets and the brooch which goes with the said necklace, both of which I received as a present on my 75th birthday and I have no other bequest to my said daughter because she is otherwise well provided for and by her technical qualifications able to provide for herself.

Melanie did not restrict herself to analysing her children. She wanted none other than herself to be the supervisor when they were analysed by other psychoanalysts, as happened with Erich in a subsequent analysis with Winnicott – who, it should be said, declined.

Melanie's shadow also fell across the following generation. She supervised the analysis of Erich's son

Michael, who was analysed by Marion Milner, who had been analysed by Sylvia Payne, who had been analysed by Melanie. This supervision was a real mess. While Milner reported on Michael's problems, the grand-mother-supervisor Melanie made harsh comments about her son Erich who she had previously analysed. However Michael got out of this tangle, and commenced analysis with Wilfred Bion, who had also been analysed by Melanie.

Melanie was the analyst of other children in her circle of friends and acquaintances: for example the children of Ernest Jones, the leading British psychoanalyst and Sigmund Freud's "official" biographer. Apart from the children Gwenith and Mervyn, Melanie also analysed their mother, Katherine Jones. The progress of the analysis was reported to Ernest Jones, in his role as father and husband, thus creating a second layer to the relationship between Melanie and Ernest, a point of view from which the family was viewed with detachment. Little Gwenith died of pneumonia at seven and a half. Mervyn's analysis was concluded satisfactorily, as Jones wrote to Sigmund Freud, who had been sceptical about Klein's approach.

In the history of psychoanalysis, it is well known that other fathers analysed their children. For example Karl Abraham, one of the principal exponents of classical psychoanalysis, analysed his daughter Hilda and used his observations in his studies into the development of the libido. Hilda behaved strangely: she was inattentive and was continually daydreaming. Then the father discovered that his daughter, who was only just seven years old, was masturbating. Hence he pointed out to her that "she should not do this, because she would not be able to go to sleep in the evening, and in the morning she would be tired and therefore not as lively and alert as the other children in school." Abraham's notes from 1913 reveal that he encouraged his daughter to tell her fantasies and noted with gratification "a first-class understanding of psychoanalysis" on Hilda's part. "She then went on to ask me – as so many patients do – if I had heard something of the same nature from other people and what I had given them for it. I told her that people felt better when they voiced their thoughts to the doctor, and then they could lie peacefully in their beds at night."

Hilda, in turn, became a psychoanalyst and told the story of her analysis under her father in the biography she wrote about him. Amongst other things, she recalls the episode of the tonsillectomy described in Abraham's notes, now referred to as *Little Hilda*. Hilda was not informed of the coming operation. At the surgery, two nurses suddenly appeared, one of whom held her still on her lap while they anaesthetised her. Hilda screamed and continued to scream during her sleep in the days to come. The father noted down that, after the operation, his daughter had become "very awkward" about those nightmares. Referring to this period, Hilda commented with annoyance:

> He failed to see this as a normal re-enactment of the terror I had felt, nor did he seem to appreciate the castration anxiety that had been described in Freud's early works applied only to boys, though it was acknowledged that girls felt penis envy.

Hilda therefore turned it into a question of the correct analytical interpretation: it was fear of castration and not tonsillectomy itself, as it was once practised.

I too can remember an identical scene in Livorno during the fifties. My parents took me to the doctor without telling me anything beforehand. I was wrapped in a long bandage so that my hands could no longer move. A nurse held me still on his knees, and then a retractor appeared to keep my mouth firmly open. A little bit of anaesthetic in the mouth, a sizeable pair of forceps, and out it came! After that, I was terrified and tearful every time I went by the surgery door (which is still there to this day). My father, who was not a psychoanalyst, could not provide any psychoanalytical explanation that I would later be able to examine and criticise, so now when I read Abraham's interpretation and Hilda's correction, I begin to wonder myself about those nightmares of mine.

Let us move on to Carl Jung, who referred to the analysis of his daughter Agathli in two letters to Sigmund Freud in 1909. As was their custom, Jung introduced the case as though it did not concern his daughter: "About the time when Freud published his report on the case of 'Little Hans', I received from a father who was acquainted with psychoanalysis a series of observations concerning his little daughter, then four years old." The child, who is given the name of Anna, proves to be very curious about sexual matters and the father goes as far as to provide her with very complete explanations. In his article *Psychic Conflicts in a Child* (1910), Jung also reports on his other and younger daughter Gretl, and her questions. Anna Freud's biographer Young-Bruehl observes that Jung gave the two girls the names of Freud's daughters, Anna and Sophie: just as Sophie was jealous of the birth of Anna, so Agathli was jealous of Gretl. Jung was cautious about the imposition of preconceived ideas onto the material provided during the conversations with the young girl, and he was also more prudent about the pedagogic application of psychoanalysis:

> We should try to see children as they really are, and not as we would wish them; that, in educating them, we should follow the natural path of development, and eschew dead prescriptions.

Chapter 3
Patients and lovers

In 1907 Minna Bernays is supposed to have told Carl Gustav Jung that she was having an affair with her brother-in-law Sigmund Freud, and Jung did not fail to spread this news (first in an interview in 1957 and then in the printed word in 1969). Having become entangled in a complicated love affair with his Russian patient Sabina Nikolaevna Spielrein, Jung could now claim that the founding father of psychoanalysis was no better, having had a secret love affair with his sister-in-law. Thus the myth of Freud's sexual abstinence crumbled and the notorious polygamy of his heretical pupil Jung appeared less remarkable.

When considering the sexual and romantic affairs of Freud, Jung and a multitude of other psychoanalysts, it should first be made clear that critics have adopted two distinct approaches. The first perceives these particular aspects of private life as wholly irrelevant to the history of psychoanalysis. Exponents of this approach argue that those who put importance on such things do so out of sensationalism and a desire to defame psychoanalysis in general. According to some, such motivations lurk behind the attempt to prove a relationship between Sigmund Freud and his sister-in-law Minna – who is thought to have aborted the result of this affair – by even sifting through lists of hotels and spas in Tyrol, where the lovers supposedly lived in 1900. The desire to denigrate the founder of psycho-analysis is also betrayed by another bit of gossip: in the Vienna flat, you could enter Minna's bedroom only by a door directly linked to that of Sigmund and his wife Martha.

Maliciousness and gossip have always been contemptuously rejected, particularly by Freud himself who, according to an account gathered by Paul Roazen, resentfully responded to one of his patients: "So you believe in my famous love affair with Minna." However, some people went further and subjected these rumours to a psychoanalytical interpretation. For example, Kurt Eissler, a fierce defender of Freud's good name, suggested a "psychoanalysis of the lie" for the Minna-Sigmund affair. Eissler has always jealously guarded the correspondence and documents of the founding father of psychoanalysis in the Library of Congress. Given that this material will not be available for many decades, Paul Roazen's subtle irony appears fitting and entirely justified: "Josef Breuer [one of the first of Freud's co-workers] must have had something interesting to say for a letter to be sealed until 2102". What can it be that could possibly be so shocking to cyberspace readers in the next century?

On the other hand, those who follow the second approach feel that the private lives of psychoanalysts, especially the early leading exponents, are an important source for understanding the theoretical and therapeutic development of psychoanalysis. The problems of transference and counter-transference – according to this view – originate in these awkward relationships between analysts and patients. Psycho-analysts would develop concepts to deal with such complex relationships as and when they had to encounter and overcome them (according to Aldo Carotenuto, Jung formulated the concepts of Anima, Animus and Shadow as a result of his relationship with Spielrein).

Here I will follow a third approach, which should not be understood in either a moralistic or slanderous sense. I wish to demonstrate that sexual relations between patient and analyst represent an important feature of the history of psychoanalysis. These relationships were not simply "accidents" through which psychoanalysts were able to strengthen psychoanalysis' defences against scabrous situations, nor were they simply the gratification of sexual desire, abetted by the couch and the suffused light of a psychoanalyst's office. On the other hand, sexual relationships between analyst and patient, and their frequent development into marriages appear to be a recurring and fundamental component of the history of psychoanalysis, while this is much less the case in any of the other branches of psychology, psychotherapy and psychiatry. To dismiss "love affairs" (Farber and Green) between analysts and patients as mere gossip is to fail to understand the historical role of sexual practice and emotional ties with patients in the foundation of psychoanalysis.

Before discussing the reasons for this recurring situation, which psychoanalysts themselves consider morally and professionally unacceptable, we should look at some of the better-known examples.

Jung is supposed to have acknowledged his own polygamy by engaging with the ideas of Otto Gross, who was under his care at the Burghölzli Hospital in Zurich. In a letter to Freud, Jung said that he saw Gross as his twin ("I discovered many aspects of my own nature, so that he often seemed like my twin brother"). Gross was certainly a fascinating character because of both his flamboyant lifestyle and the complexity of his mental disorders, but what Jung perhaps found most interesting was his explicit declaration that he wanted to destroy the barrier that separated patient from therapist.

> Dr Gross tells me that he puts a quick stop to the transference by turning people into sexual immoralists. He says the transference to the analyst and its persistent fixation are mere monogamy symbols and as such symptomatic of repression. The truly healthy state for the neurotic is sexual immorality.

Otto, who was the son of Hans Gross, one of the leading criminologists of the period, graduated in medicine and obtained the post of ship's doctor on the route between Hamburg and Latin America. He was soon taking cocaine and morphine on a regular basis, to the point where it became necessary to seek treatment at Burghölzli for detoxification and help with the psychotic symptoms.

Apart from Gross, several figures of the time ended up in a mental hospital, as Richard Noll wrote in his essay on Jung: "Switzerland and southern Germany became the home of these neopagan, sun-worshiping, nudist, vegetarian, spiritualist, sometimes anarchist, sexually liberated groups experimenting with new lifestyles or a new experience-based philosophy of life." By persistently associating strict diets and strenuous walks through the mountains with hard drugs and the hallucinated contemplation of the sun, it was predictable that some people were going to lose their minds, even if they were psychiatrists.

After his therapy, Gross also became a psychotherapist. Initially he had been involved in traditional psychiatry (he had worked in Munich for Emil Kraepelin, the founder of German academic psychiatry), but later he became enthusiastic about psychoanalysis and attempted to combine the concepts of classical psychiatry with Freud's new ideas. It seems that, for the period, his efforts were of interest, at least if we are to believe Ferenczi, who wrote to Freud about a book Gross had written. ("There is no doubt that, among those who have followed you up to now, he is the most significant." But in the same letter of 22 March 1910, Ferenczi added: "Too bad he had to go to pot"). Freud was in fact concerned that Gross's behaviour and ideas would put psychoanalysis in a bad light. By that time Gross had become professor of psychopathology in Graz and would analyse patients of some standing, such as Vittorio Benussi – who in turn was to introduce Cesare L. Musatti to psychoanalysis, and Musatti was to become one of the most famous Italian psychoanalysts of the twentieth century.

Gross was causing consternation on two fronts. His romantic connections broke all the rules and were carried on for all the world to see. Even though he was married, Gross had a relationship with both the Von Richtofen sisters: Else was married to the economist Edgar Jaffé and Frieda to the philosopher Ernest Weekley (after she divorced Ernest, Frieda was to marry D.H. Lawrence, and would recall Otto in her memoirs, in which she gave him the name Octavio). It would take an entire chapter to describe the constellation around Gross, so I will restrict myself to a few facts. In the same year, Otto had two sons, one by his wife Frieda and one by Else Von Richtofen. To avoid confusion, they were given the same name, with the blessing of the famous sociologist Max Weber, who on this occasion was the godfather but in the past had been the professor-and-lover of Else, who had also been a lover of Max's brother, Alfred. Frieda Gross was a close friend of Else and Frieda Von Richtofen, and Marianne, Max Weber's wife, was equally friendly. The other disturbing thing about Gross, which led to him being interrogated by the police, was that he allegedly assisted at least two women with their suicides – two militant anarchists, Lotte Chattemer in 1906, and Sophie Benz in 1911.

Gross interspersed a second therapy at Burghölzli, analysis under Wilhelm Stekel, and repeated treatments in psychiatric clinics with the disorderly lifestyle he led amongst the anarchists who frequented the cafés of Munich and Berlin. He ended his days as a tramp (abandoned like a crucified Christ, as Kafka who knew him was to write of his death). His life constituted an unending scandal for the new profession of psychotherapy. In particular, he caused Jung to have second thoughts about his own behaviour. However, while he was dealing with the Gross case, Jung decided that it would be best not to flaunt his relationship with his patient. He felt it would be more appropriate to keep the affair with Sabina Spielrein quiet than to change the relationship in any fundamental way.

It was also a relationship covered and obscured by various layers of interpretation. At the first level there is the historical reality. At the second level, we find the version that Jung initially gave to Freud and then the one that emerged from a three-cornered exchange of letters and opinions between Jung, Freud and Sabina herself. At the third level, there is the subsequent reconstruction of events by Aldo Carotenuto in his book *A Secret Symmetry* (1980). Finally at the fourth level, there is the the interpretation of the interpretations, i.e. the response to the documentation and Carotenuto's interpretation that came from psychoanalysts of the Jungian and Freudian schools, like Bruno Bettelheim.

The different levels have often become confused, as commonly happens in the history of psychoanalysis, where historical reality, psychological reality and interpretative reality all become wrapped up into one. It is then no surprise that, within this interpretative outlook, where interpretation takes precedence over the search for "truth", questions such as whether Carl Gustav Jung and Sabina really made love or their relationship was merely one of words and sighs are considered reductive and marginal.

It is my impression, having read the documents, that it was what is called a carnal relationship. However, what is most striking about the Sabina affair is not so much the private aspects of her relationship with Carl Gustav, as his intellectual and moral ability to separate the private from the public, and present Sabina as an objective clinical case uncontaminated by the interpersonal therapist-patient dimension.

In 1907 Jung presented the First International Congress of Psychiatry with a report entitled *The Freudian Theory of Hysteria* (Freud wrote to Jung saying that the lecture "will be a milestone in history"), which included a case of "psychotic hysteria", namely the story of Sabina, who went to Burghölzli on 17 August 1904 and remained there until 1 June 1905. The style in which the patient's story is told recalls the clinical files of traditional psychiatry: cold, neutral, the patient as an object. This account has been published several times in reconstructions of the Jung-Spielrein-Freud triangle, but sufficient attention has never been devoted to the complete absence of empathy and emotional involvement of the kind that Greenson was to consider essential in relation to his own patients (but Greenson was probably already thinking about Marilyn). Jung wrote of this relationship:

> I think a concrete example from my own experience will illustrate the meaning of Freud's teachings better than any theoretical formulations, which, because of

the complexity of the subject, are all apt to sound uncommonly ponderous.

The case is one of psychotic hysteria in an intelligent young woman of twenty. The earliest symptoms occurred between the third and fourth year. At that time the patient began to keep back her stool until pain compelled her to defecate. Gradually she began to employ the following auxiliary procedure: she seated herself in a crouching position on the heel of one foot, and in this position tried to defecate, pressing the heel against the anus. The patient continued this perverse activity until her seventh year. Freud calls this infantile perversion anal eroticism.

The perversion stopped with the seventh year and was replaced by masturbation. Once, when her father smacked her on the bare buttocks, she felt distinct sexual excitement. Later she became sexually excited when she saw her younger brother being disciplined in the same way. Gradually she developed a markedly negative attitude towards her father.

Puberty started when she was thirteen. From then on fantasies developed of a thoroughly perverse nature which pursued her obsessively. These fantasies had a compulsive character: she could never sit at table without thinking of defecation while she was eating, nor could she watch anyone else eating without thinking of the same thing, and especially not her father. In particular, she could not see her father's hands without feeling sexual excitement; for the same reason she could no longer bear to touch his right hand. Thus it gradually came about that she could not eat at all in the presence of other people without continual fits of compulsive laughter and cries of disgust, because the defecation fantasies finally spread to all the persons in her environment. If she was corrected or even reproached in any way, she answered by sticking out her tongue, or with convulsive laughter, cries of disgust, and gestures of horror, because each time she had before her the vivid image of her father's chastising hand, coupled with sexual excitement, which immediately passed over into ill-concealed masturbation.

At the age of fifteen, she felt the normal urge to form a love relationship with another person. But all attempts in this direction failed, because the morbid fantasies invariably thrust themselves between her and the very person she most wanted to love. ...

At eighteen, her condition had got so bad that she really did nothing else than alternate between deep depressions and fits of laughing, crying, and screaming. She could no longer look anyone in the face, kept her head bowed, and when anybody touched her, she stuck her tongue out with every sign of loathing.

In spite of the detached tone, however, Sabina had, according to Carotenuto, already captured Jung's heart, at least at an unconscious level. There followed Jung's letters to Freud with references, pretences and retractions in relation to this controversial reality. Sabina then became a psychoanalyst (one of her patients was Jean Piaget), and she wrote a few important articles on psychoanalytical theory and clinical practice. She returned to Russia, first to Moscow and later Rostov on the Don, where she was born, and there she died with her two daughters during the German occupation. She was murdered by the Nazis, while her brother Isaac, one of the most eminent Soviet psychologists, disappeared into a Stalinist gulag.

Sabina, a woman hated as a Jew, was loved by Jung for being one. "He told me that he loved Jewish women", she wrote in her diary, "that he wanted to love a dark Jewish girl."

On 11 September 1910, we find the following note:

> Our love grew out of a deep spiritual affinity and common intellectual interests. 'What intelligent eyes!' he sometimes sighed, or tears came to his own eyes when I explained something about, for example, Wagner's psychological music, for he had thought, felt, written (in unpublished works, too) the very same things. And I was ready to die for him, to sacrifice my honour to him. It was my first love. Not to live with him, or at least for him, for the child I wanted to give him, seemed impossible. I wrote poems for him, composed songs about him, thought only of him day and night.

On 7 March, Jung had already informed Freud of this love, but in accordance with the usual version provided by the therapist who is careful about his professional propriety:

> A complex is playing Old Harry with me: a woman patient, whom years ago I pulled out of a very sticky neurosis with unstinting effort, has violated my confidence and my friendship in the most mortifying way imaginable. She has kicked up a vile scandal solely because I denied myself the pleasure of giving her a child. I have always acted the gentleman towards her, but before the bar of my rather too sensitive conscience I nevertheless don't feel clean, and that is what hurts the most because my intentions were always honourable.

In that period, Jung had under analysis two other women who were important in his life, his wife Emma and Toni Wolff. Very soon this was to become a famous *ménage à trois*, which was tolerated by the family, probably because "The prerequisite for a good marriage," Jung wrote to Freud in a letter of 30 December 1909, "is, it seems to me, the license to be unfaithful." I will not go into the influence of these two women on Jung's psychological growth here. In this approach, the women (called *Jungfrauen*, "virgins", but the German term could also mean "Jung's women") are not seen as individual human beings of flesh and blood, but as the ghostly figures who make up Jung's psychological life: each fulfils a function and each takes up a position in Jung's psyche. If you believe the most recent biographies of Jung, there were a great many *Jungfrauen*, all committed to working with the great psychologist on his scientific projects from the early research in Zurich on word associations. Ester Aptekmann was one of these. This young Russian "was once one of my friend's patients and now she is 'one of the many'," Sabina wrote in her *Diary*. "He told me she was not one of those he could love. She has no inkling of my position vis-à-vis him, she does not even know that I have anything to do with him now. She loves him and believes that he loves her. 'Blessed is the one who can believe.' In his letters to her he uses the salutation, 'My dear colleague'!"

In other words, the patients became professional assistants and a constellation of women was formed around Jung, with whom he had romantic and professional links: Jung analysed Toni Wolff, a professional assistant and lover who became a psychoanalyst and analysed Barbara Hannah, author of a key biography of Jung, but Barbara was also analysed by Emma, Jung's wife, and so on (Fig. 3). Nadia Neri has pointed out that these important female figures in the Jung network were "all women from well-off and often aristocratic families, who in any case belonged to the cultural élite of early-twentieth-century society. They were laden with suffering and conflict, and saw analysis as an opportunity for understanding and a means of achieving sensibility and possibly even emancipation." With a few exceptions, they were not married and they did not have children.

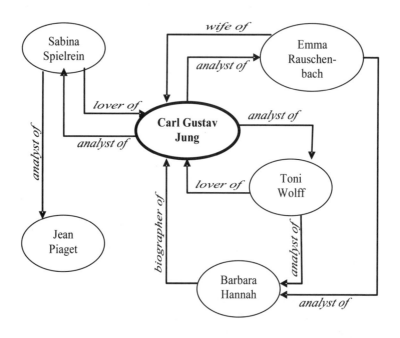

Fig. 3. The constellation for Carl Gustav Jung

Freud was also surrounded by women: the women in his family (his wife Martha, his sister-in-law Minna and his daughter Anna) and his "ladies-in-waiting", whose characteristics were unmistakable. According to Paul Roazen, "these women were either unmarried or separated, or their husbands were somehow not important," as was the case with Eva Rosenfeld, Jeanne Lampl de Groot, Marianne Rie Kris, Dorothy Burlingham and Princess Marie Bonaparte. These women were intelligent, rich and loyal: at least one of these qualities was required in order to enter the restricted circle of the two mentors.

The dedication of these vestal virgins of psycho-analysis rarely gave way to bad feeling. Of course it was felt that women were dangerous and you had to be very careful: "The way these women manage to charm us with every conceivable psychic perfection until they have attained their purpose is one of nature's greatest spectacles," Freud wrote in a letter to Jung dated 7 June 1909 on the subject of rebellious and ungrateful female patients. The analyst's work is extremely risky, the founding father added in another letter to Jung dated 18 June 1909: "In view of the kind of matter we work with, it will never be possible to avoid little laboratory explosions. Maybe we didn't slant the test tube enough, or we heated it too quickly. In this way we learn what part of the danger lies in the matter and what part in our way of handling it."

It seems to me that psychoanalysts have not sufficiently questioned what Freud meant by the test tube that is inclined too little or heated too much, or the material which in handling becomes so dangerous.

The triangle made up of Carl Gustav, Emma and Toni was the model for another emotional and professional entanglement. It has also only recently come to light, thanks to two splendid biographies, centred respectively on the male figure, the famous personality psychologist Henry A. Murray and on the female figure, his lover and assistant Christiana Morgan. The lives of Henry and Christiana seem to belong to a fantasy world that runs parallel to that of the scientific research for which Murray became famous (thanks in part to Christiana, with whom he created the Thematic Apperception Test in 1935, one of the most widely used projective tests for studying the personality). At the same time, Christiana produced dreams and visions in a state of trance that for a few years were the subject of seminars held by Jung in Zurich. Christiana typically remained in the shadows, even though she was the inspiration of Murray's and Jung's work.

The Murray family (Henry, called Harry, and his wife Josephine Rantoul, called Jo) were friendly with the Morgan family (Christiana Councilman and her husband William, called Will), partly because of the links that the Morgans had established with the other Murray family (Henry's brother Cecil, called Ike, and his wife, Veronica). These were consolidated by the brief but intense romantic relationship between Christiana and Cecil. When the two Murray families and the Morgans were on a study trip to Europe, Henry visited Jung at his home in Küsnacht and he came away profoundly impressed. At that meeting in 1925, Henry managed to express his as yet ill-defined desires and his incipient passion for Christiana. Every day for more than three weeks, Murray and Jung met and exchanged their experiences, doubts and confusions. One day when returning from a boat trip on Lake Zurich where they had visited the symbolic tower that Jung had had built at Bollingen, Murray was greeted at the house by Emma and Toni Wolff: thus he discovered the triangle that had been kept secret in Zurich and was to remain secret for many decades to come. In a climate of familial calm, the two women and their man Carl Gustav Jung had tea with Henry. While talking about Christiana, Carl Gustav and Henry agreed that the young woman would have benefited from analysis, and in the end Jung agreed to be Christiana's analyst. The sessions started in September 1925.

In his autobiography Henry recalled how on one occasion, as he took his leave of Jung, he felt like a "man reborn". Now he was ready to free his unconscious and his creativity, but above all to consummate his love for Christiana. The two families went to Florence and during a visit to the San Domenico Convent in Fiesole, Henry declared himself to the young woman in the cloister. In the summer of 1926, while Christiana was under analysis with Jung in Zurich, the Morgan and Murray families visited the master, and the visit threw light on the profound motives that allow more than one romantic liaison to coexist. Murray's biographer, Forrest Robinson, evokes that decisive moment of truth, basing himself on an interview with the American psychologist in 1970:

Will [Christiana's husband] met with Toni Wolff, who explained how it was with lovers like Harry and Christiana. He was terribly shaken but acquiesced and did his best to remain on friendly terms with his rival. Jo had a meeting of her own with Jung. Harry brought her to the tower in Bollingen, where Jung suggested that she join him on a walk along the lake. They sat and talked for a while, no more than twenty minutes or so. Jung insisted that Harry was no more a model of purity than other men. We are all part animal, he said. Marriage had once been Harry's ideal, but that phase had now passed. His love for Jo was enduring, but Christiana was also important to him, not least in relation to his work. The animal in men had been a burden to women for centuries, he assured her. It was an old story. Jo came away with the impression that Jung was a dirty old man. She was of course upset, and she protested that the meeting had been a waste of time. But Jung's characterisation of the affair as base, but typically so, seems to have helped Jo to accept it. She agreed, as Will had, that divorce was out of the question.

The relationship between Christiana and Harry was overwhelming. Christiana would occasionally persist in demanding that he divorce his wife Jo, but it was precisely because of Jo's compliance that for decades the triangle remained stable and hidden from the academic community (only a few colleagues who were also friends knew about the affair). Christiana used prearranged signs to communicate in public:

Red Bracelet = I want your body. *Sapphire Pendant* = I have something to tell you. *Navaho Necklace* = I want to help with therapeutic problems. *Red beads* = I love you very much but do not need you – Play, talk, etc. *White* = I am tired, quiet, depressed. I want your arms. *Gold necklace* = I am exultant but do not need you. *Navajo metal bands* = I am working at the Clinic, everything is fine. I do not need you. *Nothing* = domestic troubles.

Initially Henry and Christiana met secretly, using the most surprising subterfuges and stratagems. Then Henry decided to build a tower similar to Jung's. There they took refuge and made love. There Henry wrote his works of psychology and Christiana had her visions, which she wrote down and illustrated in drawings that have been preserved. The tower had three floors, designated for the three different moments in the lovers' lives: the ground floor for meditation, visions, mystical and erotic rituals, and the unconscious; the middle floor for lovemaking and the body; and the upper floor for study, intellectual research and the spirit. The three floors were illuminated in different ways: from the low lighting of the ground floor to the powerful lighting of the upper floor, reflecting the darkness of the unconscious and the illumination of the conscious mind.

Christiana noted down everything that happened in the tower in diaries and notebooks: in these accounts she calls herself Wona, and Henry takes the name of Mansol, the names that they used in their private encounters. There were highs and lows in the emotional and sexual relations between Wona and Mansol. They both had other lovers: Henry, at a certain stage, found himself managing a complex entanglement of his wife Jo, his lover Christiana and his second lover Eleanor Jones, while Christiana was having a turbulent relationship with a philosophy student called Ralph Eaton. Ralph attempted to escape his desperate love for Christiana by going through analysis with Jung in Zurich, but on his return to the United States he was rejected by Christiana and committed suicide.

Amongst the friendships, platonic loves and physical loves, Christiana had profound relationships with a considerable number of men, some of whom were very distinguished, such as the future and first president of the state of Israel Chaim Weizmann, the philosopher and mathematician Alfred North Whitehead, and the sociologist Lewis Mumford.

In 1962 Jo died suddenly of a heart attack. Christiana thought that finally she would be able to marry Henry, who instead temporised and felt that it would be more appropriate to keep their relationship secret. Christiana had started to drink increasingly heavily, and this behaviour made it easier for Henry to vacillate. In March 1967, while on holiday in the Virgin Islands, the relationship between Wona and Mansol came to its tragic end. Henry fell asleep on the beach and Christiana went into the sea. When he awoke, Henry looked around and saw Christiana's body bobbing on the water. He tried to resuscitate her mouth-to-mouth, but without success. This was one of

75

the versions of Christiana's death, because Henry himself provided more than one. Some people spoke of suicide. For others it was an accident. Some felt that it was in any case a tragic death towards which Christiana had been gradually driven by the continual frustrations and disillusionment that Henry had caused her. Mumford, who refused to go to the funeral, was of this opinion. Henry appeared deeply affected by Christiana's passing, but two years later on 17 May 1969, he married again at the age of sixty-six and his bride Nina Chandler was twenty-seven years younger than him. A year before in an interview for *Psychology Today*, he had declared: "I am a species of Pagan, or polytheist, who can't bear to think of a male-monopolised heaven."

Murray had been under analysis with Jung in Zurich, then with Franz Alexander in Boston and Chicago, and later still with Hanns Sachs in Boston. Christiana had shared analysts with Henry: Jung and Sachs. Hence the entanglements became more and more complex in the Jungian circle, just as with the Freudian one. Alexander had been analysed by Sachs, a member of the "Secret Committee", a group of loyal disciples of Freud that was founded to defend psychoanalysis. Then Alexander analysed Oliver, the son of Sigmund Freud. One of the members of the Secret Committee was Sándor Ferenczi, the founder of the Hungarian school of psychoanalysis. Ferenczi analysed other future authoritative psychoanalysts, such as Melanie Klein, Geza Roheim, Michael Balint and Eugénie Sokolnicka, all of whom feature in this book.

Sándor Ferenczi was at the centre of a complex constellation of analysts, patients and lovers (Fig. 4). Sigmund Freud had wanted Ferenczi, his "Paladin and

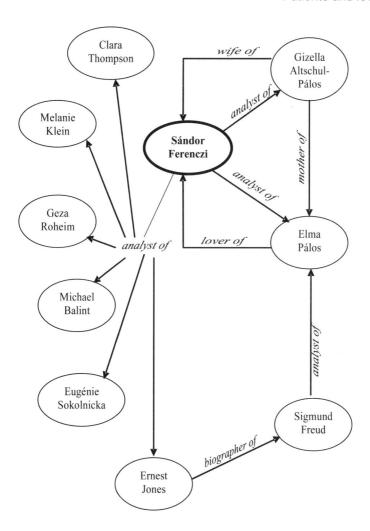

Fig. 4. Constellation for Sándor Ferenczi

secret Grand Vizier", as he called him in a letter of 1929, to marry his daughter Mathilde. Although Ferenczi chose another companion, Freud's role was still decisive. In 1900 Ferenczi met Gizella Altschul, who was married to but already separated from Géza Pàlos. She had two daughters: Elma and Magda, who was married to Ferenczi's younger brother Lajos. In a letter of 26 October 1909, Ferenczi confides to Freud that Isolde (the name used to disguise Gizella) has filled his life: "Evidently I have too much in her: lover, friend, mother, and, in scientific matters, a pupil, i.e., the child – in addition, an extremely intelligent, enthusiastic pupil, who completely grasps the extent of the new knowledge." Suddenly Gizella, who was eight years older than Ferenczi, started analysis under him. In 1911 Elma, Gizella's daughter, fell into a state of depression because her fiancé had committed suicide on her account. Her mother then advised her daughter to be analysed by her lover Ferenczi. Freud, who was duly informed by Ferenczi in a letter of 20 July 1911, expressed some doubts: "I wish you much practical success in the new enterprise with Fräulein Elma, but, of course, I fear that it will go well up to a certain point and then not at all. While you're at it, don't *sacrifice* too many of your secrets out of an excess of kindness."

The master was not mistaken, because Sándor Ferenczi fell in love with Elma: he was 38, she was 24. Sigmund got in contact with Gizella: Sándor is fundamentally a homosexual, but in order to repulse this latent condition he wants to have a child, and his hatred of his own mother, now identified with Gizella, drives him to take revenge and prefer the daughter Elma to the mother. The mother cannot have any more children and perhaps – according to Freud's interpretation – Ferenczi harbours the same hatred for her that he felt for his sister Gizella (who had the same name!). Let us not forget that the sister was linked to a childhood trauma involving the fear of castration: at the age of three years, while he was touching his little sister, Sándor was caught by the cook who, knife in hand, made him realise what would happen to him if he were to persist.

Moreover, Gizella also threatened castration if Sándor Ferenczi did not desist from his relationship with Elma. It must however have been a short-lived episode, because Gizella came to accept the relationship as long as the two were happy. Gizella "has recovered from the heavy blow and has joyfully placed herself in the service of our happiness," Sándor wrote to Sigmund on 30 December 1911. But just two days later, on 1 January 1912, Sándor decided that the relationship with Elma could not go on and had been a mistake. He asked Sigmund to continue the analysis and Sigmund accepted.

Freud very quickly pigeonholed Elma and notified Ferenczi of his "diagnosis" in a letter of 13 January 1912:

[Elma] is one of those children who, very spoiled by the father in the first few years, have felt the unavoidable loss of intimacy as neglect. It seems that all her attitudes and desires go back to this factor; hence, the yearning to show herself naked, the sexual curiosity to see something male. The breaking of the habit of masturbation in early years has already been secured; her consciousness of guilt is connected with her illicitly acquired knowledge of the male genital organs. Hence, her having to conceal, to play a role, etc. ... It's nice that she has an inclination to forget and to confuse the words for east and west in all languages except Hungarian. Her

79

second language was French: *le lever et le coucher du soleil*. The sun is naturally her father, who probably took her to bed with him in the morning, and then got up in her presence, and with whom she would like to go to bed at night. She falls in love compulsively with doctors, i.e. with persons who see her naked, physically, and now mentally.

Ferenczi's reply to Freud on 18 January is that of a confused man:

With Frau G., despite all these confirmations – despite all conscious substantiations of her attractiveness, her intellect, her spirit – I don't feel that same enthusiasm, that carefree, joyful, natural elan that Elma brought out in me. Love is irrational! ... I feel strong enough to overcome the irrational in me and am *much sooner inclined to renounce the possibility of happiness* than to subject myself and Elma to the dangers of a marriage that has *too much* risk attached to it.

On 28 February Ferenczi informed Freud that an "inner voice" had forced him to definitively break off the plan to marry Elma. On 23 April, he added that he intended to pursue the analysis with Elma himself. He enjoyed the evenings spent with Gizella and Elma "attempting to live together experimentally, in a threesome, as it were." The *ménage à trois* progressed in this manner, with Sándor managing to keep his relationship going with both Gizella who, for him, was not entirely satisfactory from a sexual point of view, and with Elma who under analysis revealed "dark drives". But then in August 1912, the psychoanalyst again broke off his sessions with Elma. A few months later, he wrote to Sigmund that his "intellectual and emotional union" with Gizella was enough for him. In 1913 Elma married an American journalist, even though her mother, according to what Sándor wrote to Sigmund, was "tirelessly championing Elma's cause with me." In 1919 Gizella married Sándor, the same day that her ex-husband died of a heart attack – "something demonic" was Freud's comment on this development, which he had himself encouraged Gizella to do.

The "Elma affair" was known to psychoanalysts, but it gained more substance with the publication of the long correspondence between Ferenczi and Freud, which as usual had been obstructed for years by Anna Freud. The letters demonstrate both the problems arising from sentimental attachments in the relationship between analyst and patient, and the complications that relations introduce into the equation: these two aspects of the Elma case intertwine in what has been defined as a kind of incest favoured by the psychoanalyst's couch.

Through his correspondence with Freud, Ferenczi conducted a kind of analysis, which was later to develop into further real sessions with the master. For Ferenczi it was certainly a process of self-meditation that he willingly accepted. Later, however, Ferenczi regretted Freud's intrusion, and accused him of having pushed him into renouncing Elma. In a letter to Georg Groddeck on 25 December 1921, Ferenczi wrote that "a fairly unfavourable comment by Freud" had induced him to leave Elma, "to fight fiercely against this love and openly reject the young woman." Yet he protested, "I want, the Id wants, not an analytical interpretation, but something real: a young woman and a child!"

Relations between Ferenczi and Freud deteriorated in later years, particularly because of the innovations the former introduced to therapeutic technique and his reassessment of seduction theory. According to Ferenczi, hysterical disorders during adulthood are based on real episodes of sexual seduction that occur during the early years of life, and not on fantasies and reconstructed beliefs, as Freud had asserted at one stage. According to the official version, supported by Ernest Jones in his biography of Freud, Ferenczi literally went mad towards the end of this life and, for this reason, adopted heterodox views in relation to Freudian doctrine – but Ferenczi's psychosis was just another of the many inventions put around by orthodox psychoanalytical circles.

Ferenczi certainly played into the hands of those who wanted to denigrate his work and standing, when he started to make some changes to his therapeutic technique in his later years. He rejected the idea that patients had to be lying down on the couch and allowed them to wander around the room and look the analyst in the face. He was willing to provide analysis free of charge more often than was considered normal. He abandoned the rule of conducting analysis always at the same place in the analyst's office, and was willing to do it in other places such as the patient's home or the analyst's holiday location. He developed the concept of "mutual analysis" whereby the patient becomes the analyst and the analyst the patient as they continuously switch roles. As though all this were not enough, he introduced the "kissing technique" – to use a malicious expression coined by Freud – that allowed patients to embrace and kiss their analyst Ferenczi, and he kept baby bottles and dolls close by, so that the patients could feel at ease when they were evoking and reliving their childhood.

When Freud came to know that the American patient Clara Thompson was boasting that she kissed her analyst, "daddy Ferenczi", the founding father wrote him this letter dated 13 December 1931 (this is the "revised" version that appears in Jones's biography of Freud):

> I see that the differences between us have come to a head in a technical detail which is well worth discussing. You have not made a secret of the fact that you kiss your patients and let them kiss you. ... Now picture what will be the result of publishing your technique. There is no revolutionary who is not driven out of the field by a still more radical one. A number of independent thinkers in matters of technique will say to themselves: why stop at a kiss? Certainly one gets further when one adopts 'pawing' as well, which after all doesn't make a baby. And then bolder ones will come along who will go further to peeping and showing - and soon we shall have accepted in the technique of analysis the whole repertoire of the *demiviergerie* and petting parties, resulting in an enormous increase of interest in psychoanalysis among both analysts and patients.

Two days later, Ferenczi replied to Freud asserting that every precaution had been taken so that these expressions of affection did not go beyond the required purpose, which was to create a calm atmosphere for analysis. This immediate reply somehow reflected Freud's request at the end of the letter "to listen to a brutal father's admonishment." In fact Sigmund had started to call Sándor "son" during their correspondence at the time of the relationship with Elma. The father therefore dutifully interfered in the son's private and public affairs precisely in his role as father.

Ferenczi's constellation overlapped with that of Michael Balint, who was well known for his theoretical and methodological innovations in the therapeutic field and for his original formulation of the doctor-patient relationship in psychological terms. Balint's first wife, Alice, was the daughter of the psychoanalyst Wilma Prosnitz Kovacs, who had been analysed by Ferenczi. After the death of Alice's father, Wilma married the architect Frederic Kovacs, who had been analysed by Georg Groddeck, author of the famous *Book of It*. Balint entered analysis first with Sachs, then with Max Eitingon, and later still with Ferenczi, his mother-in-law's ex-analyst. Michael emigrated to the United States following the death of Alice, and married an ex-patient, Edna Oakeshott, who also became a psycho-analyst. Then Michael moved to London where he met his third wife, Enid Albu-Eichholtz, who had already been analysed by Donald W. Winnicott, and was also a psychoanalyst. Enid and Michael separated after a few years, but continued to work together on important and innovative projects to integrate medicine and psychoanalysis.

Sándor Radó, a Hungarian psychoanalyst who emigrated to the United States in 1931, was involved in even more complex analyst–patient relationships. Sándor was analysed in Vienna by Erzsebet Revesz, who had been analysed by Freud. He fell in love with her, got divorced and married her. After moving to Berlin, where he started analysis under Karl Abraham, Sándor met Felix and Helene Deutsch. Felix had been Sigmund Freud's doctor and Helene had been analysed by the founding father of psychoanalysis and later became a psychoanalyst herself. At the time, Helene was also being analysed by Karl Abraham. Felix treated Erzsebet, who was seriously ill, and Sándor formed a romantic attachment with Helene. It did not last. Radó, according to a later account by Helene Deutsch, reported by Roazen in his biography of this psychoanalyst, was ...

a 'seducer of women'. ... He got gratification from conquering women, and even took pleasure in breaking up marriages; she [Helene Deutsch] claimed he liked to torture women by making them jealous and betraying them to others. Although he was not physically attractive, part of Radó's appeal to women, which mobilised their sexuality, was the intensity of his desire. ... Radó loved good food, had style and flair, and other women besides Helene were enchanted by him.

In short, this intrigue involved an analyst, Revesz, who married her patient, Radó, who in turn became a psychoanalyst and married his patient Emmy following the death of Revesz. But official psychoanalysis was more interested in Radó's assertions in relation to the founding father Freud than in any of his escapades as a "seducer". When Radó started to distance himself from the orthodox positions dictated by the "Professor" (Sigmund Freud), it was natural to consider him a paranoid. In a letter to her husband Felix in 1935, Helene Deutsch wrote that Radó was

... in the beginning phase of a psychosis. He is obsessed with Lampl's report [a review of Radó's work, written by Jeanne Lampl de Groot, who was very loyal to Freud]. ... The professor becomes an evil old man who wants to destroy him with his hatred. All of us around him are either crooks or mental cases under the Professor's spell and in his service, etc. There is no topic – not even the most remote – that doesn't finally lead back to this sphere of ideas.

Paranoia must have played this dirty trick on Radó in the unpleasant question of the Max Eitingon affair. Eitingon was a very loyal Freudian and a member of the Secret Committee. Radó, in a private note found amongst his papers, confirmed the rumour that Max

Eitingon was the brother of Leonid or Nahum Eitingon, an agent in the Soviet secret services who was implicated in the murders of various Russian émigrés, including Leon Trotsky and the General of the White Army, Yevgeny Miller. But who was Max Eitingon? He was extremely rich and lavish in funding the psychoanalytical movement and in helping the Freud family. He organised society evenings with famous guests, such as the Russian émigré philosopher Leon Chestov and renowned singer Nadezhda Vasilevna Plevitskaya. She was the wife of the White Army general Nikolai Skoblin, who is supposed to have been the organiser of the murder of his ex-compatriot Miller. Moreover it was allegedly Max Eitingon who, at the request of his brother, recruited the couple for Stalin's secret services. Plevitskaya claimed at the trial that, two days before the murder of Yevgeny Miller in Paris, she had been in the company of Max Eitingon, who was so fascinated by her that he had bought her a complete outfit of clothes and financed the publication of her autobiographical books. Plevitskaya was found guilty and died in prison. Subsequently this story, which appeared in a book by John J. Dziak on the history of the KGB published in 1987, proved to be only partly true, and it was not possible to confirm Max Eitingon's role as a Soviet agent, even on an indirect basis. One thing is certain: once again a part of the history of psychoanalysis is tied up with a more intricate network of suspicions, mysteries and partial historical truths.

Ferenczi was not the only one to be considered a madman by orthodox psychoanalysts, just as Radó was not the only one to be treated as a paranoid. Another of the master's "traitors", Otto Rank, who wrote *The Trauma of Birth* (1924), was considered to be mentally ill, in this case suffering from manic-depressive psychosis. Hence he was expelled from the American Society of Psychoanalysis in 1930, while psychoanalysts who had been his patients were required to undergo analysis again. Otto had married Beata Mincer, called Tola, in 1918, and she too became a psychoanalyst. Otto and Tola were frequent visitors to the Freud home, until there was a break between "father" and "son". According to Samuel Eisenstein, "Freud had considered Rank to be an obedient son, but one who was unable to grow up and achieve the stature of his father. He had rebelled and thus threatened to destroy what he had helped to create." In Paris, where Otto moved, he started to analyse the writer Anaïs Nin and fell in love with her. For Anaïs, this was her second experience of a love affair between analyst and patient. Her first analyst had been René Felix Allendy, a Parisian doctor whose couch was frequented by famous patients. Anaïs's relationships with Allendy and Rank became well known after the publication of her diary. Here again we find ourselves at the centre of the usual web of relationships. Allendy had analysed his cousin Eduardo Sanchez and Hugo Guiler, the former Anaïs's lover and the latter her husband. But Anaïs also had a passionate relationship with the writer Henry Miller (who at the time was writing *Tropic of Cancer*) and Henry's bisexual wife, June. René Allendy became embroiled in these relationships, and he was not so much interested in analysing her as whipping her buttocks. She tried to explain why he did this and what his secret desires were by quoting the analyst's own words to her: "I'll reduce you to a rag. You will crawl and do everything I bid you. I want you to abdicate – forget your pride – forget everything."

Following her analysis with Allendy, Anaïs moved on to Otto Rank. The results were predictable, as the patient recorded in her diary:

> Suddenly he kissed me, kissed me voraciously. And he made me lie under him and we kissed until we forgot ourselves again, but he knew we had to stop, yet we couldn't, and in our drunkenness I found myself drinking his sperm, too. ... I came away with the manuscript of one of his [Rank's] books, and I saw Henry [Miller] again. I said to Henry, "A woman should be nourished with nothing but sperm." And we talked psychoanalysis. And Henry said, "Get independent soon so we can begin our new life soon, soon."

But Anaïs followed Rank to New York and, before returning to Paris, became a very unusual kind of secretary: while Rank was analysing one patient, she would be having sexual relations with those who were waiting their turn for analysis. During the period between the analysis with Allendy and the one with Rank, Anaïs famously had an incestuous relationship with her father. As the bodies of the two lovers were drawing close – let's be modest and save ourselves from all the details recorded in the *Diary* – the father said to his daughter: "Bring Freud here, and all the psychologists. What could they say about this?" Anaïs held some interesting ideas about psychologists, as can be seen from her observations on Allendy, who was persuaded that she enjoyed his whippings:

> "I won't."
> "You can't help it. You can scream. Nobody pays any attention to screams in this house."
> "I don't want it because the marks will show. I don't want Hugo to see them, nor Henry either!"
> At this Allendy laid me on the bed and whipped my buttocks, hard.

But I noticed this: his penis, after all this excitement of his part – lashes, struggles, caresses of fury, kisses on the breasts – was still soft. Henry would have been already blazing. Allendy pushed my head toward it, as the first time, and then, with all the halo of excitement, threats, he fucked no better than before. His penis was short and nerveless. Voluptuary! He found it. I played a comedy. ... What amused me was to be able to deceive Allendy so deeply – psychologist!

What about Rank? This was her sententious assessment of "Doctor Rank" – as she often called him – and psychoanalysis:

After Rank, I will live only for the others, which is my joy. Psychoanalysis did save me, because it allowed the birth of the real me, who is religious. ... Psychoanalysis did save me from death. It allowed me to live, and if I leave life it will be of my own volition, as not containing the absolute. But how I still love the relative, a little nonsense and the warmth of a fire, and a fine collection of earrings, and Haydn on the phonograph, and the laughter with Eduardo, and the jokes on Mae West, and the new black wool costume with enormous sleeves and the sensual slit from throat to breast, and the bracelet and necklace of blue stone, set with stars, and the new underwear, and the new black velvet kimono, and the trunk drawer full of Henry's *Tropic of Cancer*, with my preface, and Rank's last letter, and the telephone ringing all day, and Turner's sensual voice requesting, and Emilia's short abortion of two hours, which I would not have exchanged for my superb adventure. Love.

Ernest Jones, Sigmund Freud's loyal official biographer, was one of the fiercest critics of "dissidents" who got embroiled in distasteful situations with their patients. But the case of Jones reveals a complex situation that is found elsewhere between analysts and patients. Here is a schematic example: Mr *X* is undergoing analysis with analyst *A*, while Mrs *Y*, *X*'s wife or lover, is undergoing analysis with analyst *B*. Now the analysts *A* and *B* discuss between themselves the cases of *X* and *Y*, so the analysis of *X* is influenced by knowledge of the analysis of *Y* and vice versa. Mr *X* and Mrs *Y* believe that they are developing their psychological life under analysis independently from each other, while in reality they are guided on another level they know nothing about. They are linked at this level which exists beyond their everyday relationship as spouses or lovers.

Let us apply this model. For some time Jones had a stable relationship with Loe Kann. He wasn't officially married to her, but he introduced her as his wife. Loe took morphine, so her partner Jones asked Sigmund Freud to take her on for analysis. The master accepted: "Jones brought me his wife for preliminary treatment, for which he has finally obtained her agreement", we read in a letter from Freud to Ferenczi dated 23 June 1912, "she is an extremely intelligent, deeply neurotic Jewess, whose case history is very easy to read. I will be very pleased to be able to expend much libido for her." The analysis must have been effective, as Freud was to write to Ferenczi again a year later: "I don't yet know how Jones will bear finding out that his wife, as a consequence of the analysis, no longer wants to remain his wife. Should it turn on the fact that women are more intelligent than we and are justified in subjecting us to their will?" However, there had been a problem between Ernest and Loe: Ernest had had a short fling with Lina, a nurse and friend of Loe, precisely during the period in which Loe was under analysis with Freud.

During the same period, Ernest started analysis under Ferenczi. The latter regularly informed Freud on the progress of Jones's analysis in his letters, while Freud in turn informed Ferenczi about the analysis of "Mrs Jones". Ernest feared that Ferenczi might be reporting on his analysis to Freud, and so Ferenczi asked Freud not to make the slightest reference to their correspondence when he was with Mrs Jones. When Freud was informed that Jones's analysis was going well, he felt relieved from his worry that Loe's analysis would lead to the break-up of her relationship with Jones, and remarked in a letter to Ferenczi, dated July 9, 1913.

> I am very pleased by what you write about Jones. I now feel far less guilty of complicity in the outcome of the process with his wife since I see her blooming so, now that she is free. This Loe has become extraordinarily dear to me, and I have produced with her a very warm feeling with complete sexual inhibition, as has rarely been the case before (probably owing to my age).

Having recovered her liberty, Loe was to marry the American writer Herbert Jones in Budapest in 1914, and given the succession to her bed, he was called Jones II.

Ernest Jones had had several problems with the law over sexual matters. On two separate occasions, he had been accused, perhaps unjustly, of "improper" behaviour in relation to some children, and one night he even ended up in a cell for these reasons, causing something of a stir in the local press. On another occasion, the head nurse at the London hospital where he worked claimed that he spent "too much time mapping out the anaesthesias of hysterical out-patients". Hence Ernest Jones had to resign from the hospital. He was also obliged to pay an ex-patient in order to stop her persisting with a possibly unfounded accusation that he had again been acting "improperly".

Once his relationship with Loe Kann was over, Ernest Jones famously ventured a courtship with the master's daughter Anna Freud, and failed. He then fell back upon the pianist, singer and composer Morfydd Owen: "a brilliant young Welsh musician" of great charm, as Jones was to remember his wife in his *Memoirs*. Morfydd died young, and Ernest moved onto his next marriage to Katherine Jolk three years later. This marriage was to produce four children, two of whom, along with their mother, were to undergo analysis with Melanie Klein, as we have already seen. Of the relationships that Jones had with his patients, who then became psychoanalysts, the best known case is that of Joan Riviere, "one of the most brilliant and acute minds in the English group" which was formed around Klein, according to Grosskurth. Joan's relationship with Ernest started in 1916 during analysis, and then she began analysis under Freud in Vienna.

We could continue at length to list this tendency of analysis to stray into romantic liaisons. Just to give a few examples, Margaret Mahler, who studied child psychosis, and her analyst August Aichhorn; René Laforgue, the French psychoanalyst accused of collaboration with the Nazis, and his patient Delia Clauzel; Wilhelm Reich, the author of the book *The Sexual Revolution*, and his patient, future wife and psychoanalyst, Annie Pink, known by the double-barrelled surname taken from her two husbands, Reich-Rubinstein, etc.

The psychoanalysts of Hollywood deserve a chapter all of their own, and their heterosexual and homosexual relationships with patients have often ended up in the media due to some of their tragic outcomes. Because of their number and significance, they have become the central theme of a book by Farber and Green, *Hollywood On The Couch*. One of the most scandalous was the case of the psychoanalyst David Rubinfine in 1963, who formed a relationship with his patient, the actress Elaine May, and married her six weeks after his wife Rosa had committed suicide precisely because of her distress at being abandoned by David.

Thus, when the seventy-five-year-old psychoanalyst Milton Wexler, who we have already met as one of Marilyn Monroe's therapists (he was also Jennifer Jones's), was able to achieve his life-long ambition to script a film, the plot was inevitable. In the film *The Man Who Loved Women* (1983) written together with the director Blake Edwards and his son, the beautiful psychoanalyst played by Julie Andrews goes to bed with her patient Burt Reynolds. Blake Edwards was a patient of Wexler and was married to Andrews, who in turn had been a patient of Gerald Aronson, another eminent Hollywood psychoanalyst (who had also analysed Marlon Brando and Anthony Perkins). Edwards and Andrews not only had separate analysts (as is usual in a psychoanalytical setting) but, as Farber and Green point out, they had joint sessions with both Wexler and Aronson.

The therapeutic problems arising from the analytical relationship spilling over into a sexual one constitutes a vast subject. As Glen O. Gabbard and Eva P. Lester have observed in *Boundaries and Boundary Violations in Psychoanalysis* which deals with this very theme, any attempt to treat it encyclopaedically would fill a large volume. It probably wouldn't be enough. Given that "history tends to repeat itself", the authors go on to argue, the links in the chain are self-producing. After discussing "historical" examples of this phenomenon, they move on to more recent cases and invite us to reflect on what is happening now in the analytical setting and what will happen in the future. The result is a kind of psychoanalysis of the cases of "boundary violation" during psychoanalytical sessions. Indeed, the question of "relations" between the psychoanalyst and the patient has been dealt with by psychoanalysis in terms of the transference and counter-transference dynamics. The analyst must be capable of finding a balance between "falling in love", understood as the emotional transport of the patient in relation to the analyst and "falling in love" as the prelude to sexual relations. The former type of love is necessary for the pursuance of the analysis, while the latter destroys the analysis. Analysts must in turn control their emotions in relation to the patient. Without losing their emotional involvement – this was the fundamental point for Ferenczi – they must not allow themselves to be drawn into a romantic and sexual attraction. This difficult state of love between the patient and the analyst has been usefully summarised by Robert Michels:

> The love that a patient feels for his or her therapist is therefore both inevitable and dangerous: inevitable in the development of a relationship that is indispensable for the therapy, and dangerous if the therapist does not understand its significance and responds in a counter-transferential manner (either too positively or too negatively). The positive transference response that becomes a "real" but partial and one-sided love is unhappy as a love affair and wretched as a form of therapy. The negative counter-transference response that keeps a distance and emotional detachment from the patient in order

to avoid the dangers of intimacy, may avoid dangerous liaisons but renders therapy impossible. Without this possible danger, there is no chance of any benefits. The therapist who is aware of the problems of transference and counter-transference is best placed to negotiate a solution that avoids these two undesirable outcomes.

Balanced management of transference and counter-transference does not appear to have been easy for leading figures in psychoanalysis. It sometimes appears like wishful thinking, a utopia rather than a condition which, once it has been acquired through the training process for analysts, should guide relationships with the patient. On the basis of historical documents, the impression from the outside is of a state of flux: Sigmund Freud, who personally encountered transference that was too "concrete", asserted that "transference was a cross to bear". Even the polemical observation by Wilhelm Reich (who also married one of his patients) does not go far enough. He claimed that psychoanalysts were fixated with the genital phase of the psychosexual development outlined by Sigmund Freud and therefore masturbated their patients in the area of the genitals during analysis. If this were the case, the control of patients' transference would surmount this fixation so typical of analysts. But Reich's account should be taken with a pinch of salt: he too, according to his former fellow pupils, died half mad after having developed a science-fiction theory of orgasms and orgones. For his part, Freud believed that the analyst was not supposed to accept proposals from his female patients. In *Observations on Transference-Love* in 1915, he argued:

> If the patient's advances were returned it would be a great triumph for her, but a complete defeat for the treatment. She would have succeeded in what all

patients strive for in analysis – she would have succeeded in acting out, in repeating in real life, what she ought only to have remembered, to have reproduced as psychical material and to have kept within the sphere of psychical events. ... The love-relationship in fact destroys the patient's susceptibility to influence from analytic treatment. A combination of the two would be an impossibility.

The delicate state of transference, according to Freud, can and must be reversed in favour of the analytical process itself:

It is, therefore, just as disastrous for the analysis if the patient's craving for love is gratified as if it is suppressed. The course the analyst must pursue is neither of these; it is one for which there is no model in real life. He must take care not to steer away from the transference-love, or to repulse it or to make it distasteful to the patient; but he must just as resolutely withhold any response to it. He must keep a firm hold of the transference-love, but treat it as something unreal, as a situation which has to be gone through in the treatment and traced back to its unconscious origins and which must assist in bringing all that is most deeply hidden in the patient's erotic life into her consciousness and therefore under her control.

However, the management of transference – Freud added in his *Observations* – varies from patient to patient; his suggested strategy does not apply to all patients:

There is, it is true, one class of women with whom this attempt to preserve the erotic transference for the purposes of analytic work without satisfying it will not succeed. These are women of elemental passionateness who tolerate no surrogates. They are children of nature who refuse to accept the psychical in place of the material, who in the poet's [H. Heine] words, are accessible only to "the logic of soup, with dumplings for arguments".

Having placed the sexual relationship between patient and analyst firmly within the category of "transference and countertransference", everything can then be justified after the event. We can, therefore, find justification both in terms of the development of psychoanalysis – there were unexpected events while our theory was developing but now, psychoanalysts argue, we know what they are and we know how to behave – and in terms of the individual's psychological growth which is a path full of "complications" that are, according to Freud, inseparable "from our method". The founding father of psychoanalysis had himself asserted: "No one who, like me, conjures up the most evil of those half-tamed demons that inhabit the human breast, and seeks to wrestle with them, can expect to come through the struggle unscathed."

Hence we are not allowed to make judgements about when love means transference and counter-transference. Love – a common experience – becomes an element within a theory. The theory has its own assumptions. Whether you accept them or reject them is self-referential. However, we have to ask ourselves quite simply whether this love that blossoms in an analytical situation isn't debased by the lack of what would generally be called a balanced relationship. It seems to me a very simple argument: we should respect those we fall in love with, their identity and who they really are, without swamping them with our own interpretation of life from the position of power that we exercise over their souls. This point brings to mind the words of another great exponent of psychoanalysis, Erich Fromm – who also married one of his patients, Frieda Reichmann – from his work *The Art of Loving*:

> Respect is not fear and awe; it denotes, in accordance with the root of the word (*respicere* = to look at), the ability to see a person as he is, to be aware of his unique individuality. Respect means the concern that the other person should grow and unfold as he is. Respect, thus, implies the absence of exploitation. I want the loved person to grow and unfold for his own sake, and in his own ways, and not for the purpose of serving me.

Chapter 4
Inventions and distortions

In 1915 Freud greeted the forthcoming publication of *A Young Girl's Diary* with enthusiasm in a letter to Hermine Hug-Hellmuth, who was editing the work. The book, which only came out in 1919, used his letter as its preface:

> The diary is a little gem. I really believe it has never before been possible to obtain such a clear and truthful view of the mental impulses that characterise the development of a girl in our social and cultural stratum during the years before puberty. ... It is your duty, I think, to publish the diary. My readers will be grateful to you for it.

Thanks to this presentation, the *Diary* excited a great deal of interest and was widely read. Hug-Hellmuth, who was one of the pioneers of child psychoanalysis and a member of the Viennese Psychoanalytical Society, was much admired and protected by Sigmund Freud. However, her contribution to the book proved to be much more than that of an editor. A mature woman of over forty years, she had written the diary herself and attributed it to a young girl who was making her first discoveries of her body and her mind. When the deception was discovered, the *Diary* was initially withdrawn from the bookshops, but it was later reprinted and translated into several languages. Nobody ever made it clear that it was a complete fabrication. The preface to the *Diary* appears in Freud's collected works, but even in the most recent reprints, there is no reference to the fact that it is a fake. People still continue to "repress" this episode in the history of psychoanalysis, and prefer to believe that Hug-Hellmuth was a reliable scholar of the child's mind.

This affair had both a comic and a tragic side. The comic side concerned the discovery of the deception. Paradoxically, Hug-Hellmuth was exposed by Sir Cyril L. Burt, an eminent English psychologist who had become famous precisely because of his "casual approach" to science. He had falsified the results of tests on twins in order to demonstrate that intelligence is hereditary, and had published several articles under female pseudonyms.

The tragic side was the death of Hug-Hellmuth. The "real" object of this psychoanalyst's research was in fact her nephew Rudolf Otto Hug (called Rolf), the illegitimate son of her half-sister Antonia. Rolf, who was born in 1906, had a difficult life. Following the death of his mother in 1915, he was entrusted to a governess who constantly moved house, and so his tutors also constantly changed until the last one, Isidor Sadger, who had been Hug-Hellmuth's psychoanalyst. In the end, Rolf went to live in his aunt's home, where she subjected him to endless sessions of analysis. One fine day in 1924, Rolf was surprised by his aunt while he was stealing her money. He first tried to suffocate her with a cushion and then strangled her (lastly, to make sure that she would never speak again, he stuck a handkerchief in her mouth). This murder, which ended up on the front page of newspapers, made a deep impression on public opinion and was not good publicity for psychoanalysis. Rolf spent a few years in prison, but on his release, he asked Paul Federn, president of the Viennese Psychoanalytical Society, for compensation, claiming that his criminal behaviour had been the consequence of psychoanalysis's therapeutic practices.

But if you are born a "case", you are condemned to remain one and to act out your part. Thus Rolf's demands for money were interpreted psycho-analytically as a plea for more therapy, and so he was promptly advised to start further analysis with Helene Deutsch. Rolf, however, let it be understood in his own inimitable manner (i.e. by molesting his new analyst in the street) that he would never attend her sessions. Helene's husband, Felix, engaged a private detective to protect her. The result was a kind of multiple tailing, as Lisa Appignanesi and John Forrester recount in their book *Freud's Women*: when she went out, Helene was followed by two men, the detective who tailed Rolf, and Rolf, who was hot on the heels of the woman who wanted to be his analyst.

The question of invented case studies started to stir the community from the moment the movement came into existence. In his memoirs, Jones recalled how the standing joke at the weekly meetings of the Viennese Psychoanalytical Society held at Freud's home was "Stekel's Wednesday patient". This was a humorous reference to Wilhelm Stekel's "irresponsible attitude towards the truth". Whenever anyone was talking about a certain case or argument, Stekel, one of the earliest members of Freud's circle, would immediately claim that that very day he had visited a patient with identical symptoms. As though this wasn't enough, Stekel was also in the habit of inventing events in his own personal life, and he did this in the presence of Freud:

> Another of this gentleman's unpleasant habits was to illustrate his contentions at Society meetings by quoting material from his personal life, especially his early childhood. It was mostly quite invented or else

grossly falsified, and he would defiantly glare at Freud, who of course knew the real facts from his analysis, knowing full well he would not contradict him.

Here Jones assumes that Stekel could only produce "the real facts" during his analysis with Freud, or that in any case his analyst Freud considered them to be true. Clearly it would be quite legitimate to doubt any of Stekel's accounts, if he was a well-known liar. We have to assume then that Jones thought it impossible to lie during analysis with Sigmund Freud. However, Freud must have formed a clear opinion on Stekel, both in relation to his behaviour which was immoral to say the very least (it was said that not only did he invent cases, but he also had sexual relations with his patients), and in relation to his attitudes to psychoanalytical orthodoxy: "Stekel is a swine and is incessantly inventing new unpleasantness, petty jealousies, and insults", as the master was to write to Ferenczi on 17 October 1912. A possible justification for Stekel's flights of fancy could have been the cosseted atmosphere in which the society's meetings took place every Wednesday evening. In Peter Gay's biography of Freud, we find the following account provided by Max Graf:

> The gatherings followed a definite ritual. First, one of the members would present a paper. Then, black coffee and cakes were served; cigars and cigarettes were on the table and were consumed in great quantities. After a social quarter of an hour, the discussion would begin. The last and decisive word was always spoken by Freud himself. There was an atmosphere of the foundation of a religion in that room. Freud himself was its new prophet who made the heretofore prevailing methods of psychological investigation appear superficial.

It may be that Stekel's imagination (like that of a few others) was overexcited by this atmosphere of arcane rituals for the newly initiated. The fact is that if you read the "case studies" described by Stekel, you cannot help being mesmerised by endless misgivings over their authenticity. In his *Frigidity in Women*, which was published in 1921, there is the fascinating account of "21-year-old Miss Anna" who suffered from dispareunia, that is pain in the genitals during sexual intercourse. Anna "complained that in spite of all her intimacies (with men) she has never become acquainted with the true love thrill. She achieved orgasm during masturbation, but never as the result of sexual intercourse." Stekel introduces the auto-biographical account written by Anna herself with an interesting observation that adds a novelistic dimension to her story. She was apparently "the Viennese type of 'flapper', first depicted by Arthur Schnitzler in his literary creations, then utilised also in innumerable songs, chansons, opera couplets, etc., [and] seems worthy of a psychologic analysis." He then makes the following claim for the long and absorbing autobiography: "Aside from *The Story of Little Hans*, I know no other document that furnishes us such deep insight into the true life of the child, or reveals so instructively the conflicts of a person of simple mental organisation. Even *Tagebuch eines Verlorenen* (*Diary of a Lost Soul*), or Rousseau's *Confessions* pales in comparison with this girl's helpful candour." With these references to psychological fiction rather than true autobiography, the unconscious played a trick on Stekel and the expression "helpful candour", which appears to be a lapsus, puts us on our guard.

Masturbation is remarkably common in the case studies that Stekel reports on, and at all ages: small children, teenagers, youths and old people. It seems to have been something of an obsession with Stekel and central to his clinical interests, as was sexual impotence, from which he himself suffered according to his autobiography. If the rumour that he had "relationships" with his patients was true, we have to wonder what kind of sexual behaviour he engaged in to respond to the many cases of female frigidity he encountered in his career and described in such detail in his books. Moreover, we have to ask where reality ended and fantasy started in the innumerable cases of "sexual deviation" ranging from zoophilia (the "sexual abuse of animals" according to Stekel's own definition) to paedophilia. I will avoid quoting even a few lines of these, for fear of being accused of promoting pornography. To be honest, I began to find Stekel rather disturbing from the moment I started reading these case studies, and I can understand why in psychoanalytical circles, he was nicknamed St Ekel, which in German means "St Filth". However, case study no. 109 has to be examined. It is presented as an example of narcissism ("an infatuation with and ecstatic rapture over one's self", as defined by Stekel), and it seems like a splendid plot for a novel by Schnitzler or Roth (Stekel was in fact a writer of novels, plays and children's rhymes, and according to Henri F. Ellenberger, "some of the characters in his plays and humorous short stories seem more real than the clinical cases in his psychoanalytical publications"):

> Mr J.L., thirty-nine, is able to copulate only when he can see himself performing the act. His interest in his love partner is secondary. His most ardent wish is to have the walls and the ceiling of his room covered with mirrors. He maintains a miserly existence as he saves money in the hope of fulfilling his fantasy in the grand manner. In his masturb-

ation fantasies he always sees himself in such a mirror-lined room. He usually masturbates while looking at his mirrored image.

He is a "mirror-man". He carries several pocket mirrors and holds them before his face frequently. He spends much of his waking time admiring his reflection. His stay in the bathroom in the morning is prolonged by a looking glass positioned for that purpose. He combs his hair meticulously as he views his head from every angle. With uncompromising vanity he is determined to be the most elegant man in town. He envies quick-witted men who radiate socially. He has collected a little thesaurus of "smart" sayings which he uses in his conversations. He fancies himself as the great master of repartee. He loves to tell jokes and often pretends he has authored them. He is a member of many clubs and social circles, knows all the rules of etiquette, and would be mortified if he were caught in a faux pas. He is over-gregarious. Despite his avarice, he once readily paid a high fee to get his by-line above another man's newspaper article. He, himself, never wrote a line that was published.

He remembers that his mother spent endless hours before the mirror fussing with her hairdo. The patient was a pampered only child. His parents died when he was fifteen, and he was taken into the home of an aunt who treated him with indifference. It was in this cool setting, that contrasted with the excessive warmth of his earlier life, that he developed his severe narcissism.

Stekel's "stories" were certainly striking, as Lou Andreas-Salomé pointed out in a letter to Freud on 23 February 1924: they liked his "no-nonsense approach" and "his questionable case histories are taken by people to be evidence of the truth of anything that appears before them, as though they were drugged by the ingenious haste with which he arrives at a conclusion". It was Viktor Tausk, another founding member of Freud's inner circle, who accused Stekel of deception. The two were always arguing at the meetings of the Psychoanalytical Society. Stekel and Tausk were to share the same fate of committing suicide.

Hug-Hellmuth and Stekel confronted psychoanalysis with the problem of falsified case studies. But that was not all. Recent historical research has brought up a more subtle problem. It has been asked whether other more famous cases, such as Freud's own ones on which psychoanalytical theory and therapy were based, actually reflected objective facts. In other words, were the case studies faithful accounts of patients' clinical histories and, above all, of the therapy's results, or were they "reconstructions of the events", forced interpretations, distortions of reality and a kind of fictionalised version of clinical cases? The best example of these must be Sigmund Freud's "Wolf Man". Because of its interesting implications and historical connections, I have chosen to devote the next chapter to this case. Here I will only quote a few examples of the "originality" to be found in some of the most famous of Freud's clinical cases, milestones in psychoanalytical thought.

Naturally, we start with the case of Anna O. Although it was described by Josef Breuer, this case was considered a fundamental turning-point in Sigmund Freud's therapy for hysteria and was therefore equated with the birth of psychoanalysis. Indeed, Freud's accounts of this case are of much more interest than anything that Breuer wrote. Breuer started to treat Anna O. (who, in reality, was Bertha Pappenheim, a young Viennese woman) in 1880 for symptoms that were to be defined as typical of hysteria. If we were now to describe those symptoms, the stages of the illness, the progress of the therapy and the result, we would be getting into very muddy waters indeed. The best way to deal with it is to present the "official" version of the Anna O. case, as it has come down to us in Freud's *Autobiography*:

A chance observation showed her physician that she could be relieved of these clouded states of consciousness if she was induced to express in words the affective fantasy by which she was at the moment dominated. From this discovery, Breuer arrived at a new method of treatment. He put her into deep hypnosis and made her tell him each time what it was that was oppressing her mind. After the attacks of depressive confusion had been overcome in this way, he employed the same procedure for removing her inhibitions and physical disorders.

Freud was then to abandon hypnosis in favour of the "talking cure", and discover the existence of unconscious representations that opposed their verbal and conscious expression during sessions. Psycho-analysis was born.

This evolution from hypnosis to therapy founded on verbalisation, as outlined by Freud, is so potent that it has resisted any historical revision. Of course, it may be argued that small details were not exactly as Freud claimed, but the substance never changes. Thus the case of Anna O. is important not so much for its truthful reflection of an objective and historical reality, as for the significance that it has assumed in the history of psychoanalysis. This is also true of Freud's other clinical cases, given that they document stages in the development of his thought and become fixed within a general framework of Freud's making. Significance is attributed to those aspects that confirm the logic of this evolution, while others that could undermine it are passed over or ignored. Frank

Sulloway, one of the leading authorities on the history of Freud's theories, wrote in his 1992 article on Freud's clinical cases, that for Freud's "followers" these "case histories performed a powerful ritualistic function – they became dramatic showpieces of the healing powers of psychoanalysis, of the arduous and even Herculean nature of the analytic process, and of Freud's own brilliance as an investigator and physician." Sulloway quotes the assertion by Mark Kanzer and Jules Glenn that Freud's clinical cases did nothing less than "transcend the boundaries of the clinical and assume legendary proportions as part of the human heritage."

But psychoanalysis did not restrict itself to extolling the case studies of its founding father as myths and legends. Just as psychoanalysis describes the processes of construction and reconstruction to which a patient subjects his or her own psychological content, fantasies and overall mental status, so it is also possible to perceive Freud's clinical cases as the product of a process of construction and reconstruction produced by Freud himself. The case of Anna O. appears a good example of this: Freud is supposed to have "reviewed" and "updated" his interpretations of this case on the basis of the same psychological mechanisms and processes by which any person reviews their own fantasies relating to the past. He therefore used applied psychoanalysis on the development of psychoanalysis itself. Such an approach would horrify historians of science who would undoubtedly reject a similar simplification of historical research. While historical reconstructions (including archaeology, to which Freud often referred) are subject to interpretations, revisions and reconsideration on the basis of new documents, interviews, letters etc., there is however one unalterable factor: if the archaeologist wishes to reconstruct a building of which only ruins remain, he would never think that those ruins are irrelevant to his task of reconstruction. He would not believe that they were only the cue for triggering a work of fantasy guided by the unconscious. If a historian were continuously subject to fantasies and interpretations suggested by the unconscious, he would do better to start writing novels.

In Freud's case, we are faced with a dilemma. On the one hand, we might feel that the mistakes, oversights and memory losses committed by the father of psychoanalysis when writing up his clinical cases were the fruit of his unconscious. But then we would have to say that we have another clinical case on our hands, that of "Mr. Sigmund F., Viennese doctor and inventor". On the other hand, we might conjecture, as do Henri Ellenberger and Frank Sulloway, that they were the product of a deliberate decision. Here we are talking about a genuine case of historical falsification. According to historical research (see on this point the research carried out by H.F. Ellenberger, A. Hirschmüller, P. Swales and M. Borch-Jacobsen), several elements in the case of Anna O. have been shown to be untrue. We shall just look at a few of the many uncovered in the Borch-Jacobsen book, whose original sub-title in French is significantly *A mystification that lasted a hundred years*, while in Italian it was *Psychoanalysis's first lie.*

In spite of attempts by Anna Freud, Ernest Jones and the custodians of the Freud Archives to keep intrusive and "defamatory" historians at bay, it has been possible to access documents that have cast doubts on the story of Anna O. This story may have been invented to create an ideal development from therapies based on hypnosis to analytical therapy, sacrificing any unwitting victims along the way. There was honest Breuer, accused of theoretical and therapeutic ineptitude, and subconsciously persecuted – according to the "wise" interpretations of psycho-analysis – by not one but three women symbolically linked to the same name, Bertha: his mother, his daughter and his patient. Then there was Bertha Pappenheim, who, according to the same interpretations, was supposed to have started her campaign against prostitution because of her long-standing personal problems with her sexuality and not because prostitution was an important social problem.

It is not true that to treat Bertha, Breuer used the cathartic method, which is based on recall and verbalisation of the past and release from harmful psychological perceptions that cause hysterical symptoms. He limited himself to hypnosis and the prescription of large doses of chloral and morphine.

It is not true, as claimed in *Studies on Hysteria*, that after the treatment Bertha "regained her mental balance entirely" and that "since then she has enjoyed complete health". Immediately following Breuer's treatment, Bertha had to be treated in a Swiss nursing home. Psychoanalytical handbooks also claim that the therapy was effective in all the clinical cases that were actually administered by Freud, but this was again *not true*, as has been demonstrated by historians who identified the persons he treated and investigated their lives following therapy.

It is not true that Bertha had a hysterical pregnancy while yearning to have a child by Breuer. Many enquiries into the case of Anna O. have made much of this point, particularly in relation to Freud's observation that Breuer had not understood the significance of sexuality and the transference mechanism in the relationship between patient and analyst.

It is not true that Breuer, alarmed by Bertha's sentimental involvement, stopped the therapy and fled to Venice with his wife Mathilde for a kind of second honeymoon in which his daughter Dora was conceived (Dora was conceived *earlier*, when Bertha was still undergoing therapy with Breuer).

It is not true that Mathilde attempted to commit suicide because she was jealous of Bertha. It does however appear that Bertha, who became politically and socially committed in the years that followed, preferred not to dwell on her experience of *fin de siècle* Vienna, which included hysteria, hypnosis and morphine, as well as false pregnancies and false accounts of her life. It also appears that she was not in the habit of advising psychoanalysis to anyone suffering from some psychological disorder.

Just as with Anna O., systematic investigations have been carried out over the last twenty years into the lives, before, during and after treatment, of Emmy, Lucy, Katharina, Elisabeth, Mathilde, Rosalie, and Cäcilie, the pseudonyms under which Freud hid the identities of his patients in *Studies on Hysteria*. Similar studies have also been made into the lives of Dora, the Wolf Man, the Rat Man and little Hans. These have revealed biographies that, from both a human and a psychological point of view, are richer and more complex than was suggested by Freud's clinical accounts. In spite of this, myth continues to prevail over history, as we have already seen with Bertha Pappenheim. The history is to be found only in scholarly articles written in specialist publications that are inaccessible to the average reader, whereas the myths continue to be passed down and reinforced by literature, cinema and theatre (for example the life of

Anna O. written by Lucy Freeman or Dora's experiences as portrayed on the screen).

Historians would dearly like to inspect the notes that Freud used when writing up his case studies, in order to verify which elements were selected, discarded or highlighted. Unfortunately, Freud destroyed these documents as soon as he published his accounts. However, in one case, that of the Rat Man, this material has been conserved. Thus the Canadian psychoanalyst Patrick Mahony has been able to determine how Freud "constructed" the case of the Rat Man.

Ernst Lanzer – this was the name of the Rat Man, as Mahony revealed in 1986 – was a classic psycho-analytical case. It will be no surprise, then, that when the First Congress of the International Society of Psychoanalysis in 1908 heard Freud explain this case, the audience was spellbound for five whole hours. Ernst underwent treatment with Freud from October 1907 to September 1908, or at least that is what we have been told. In reality, the analysis did not last eleven months (Freud talks of "about a year"), but systematically for only three months and then continued with increasingly infrequent sessions up to a maximum of nine and a half months. The "case of the Rat Man" is traditionally considered the most complete and rigorous in terms of its explanation and the most successful from a therapeutic point of view. Analysis concentrated on Ernst's phobia for rats, which was associated with obsessive and compulsive symptoms. While Ernst had been serving in the Imperial Army, his captain told him something that for him became a nightmare (the so-called "great obsessive fear"). The captain had been telling him about "a specially horrible punishment used in the

East", and as Ernst was literally unable to describe it, Freud asked if it was impaling:

> "No, not that ... the criminal was tied up ...," he expressed himself so indistinctly that I could not immediately guess in what position, "... a pot was turned upside down on his buttocks ... some *rats* were put into ... and they ...," he had again got up, and was showing every sign of horror and resistance ... "*bored their way in* ..." "Into his anus", I helped him out.

Freud identified the origins of Ernst's phobia through a chain of associations. As Freud's narration cannot be bettered for its literary effect, it is best to quote its essential parts. Where did this phobia of rats come from?

> His father, in his capacity as non-commissioned officer, had control over a small sum of money and had on one occasion lost it at cards (thus he had been a 'Spielratte' [literally 'play-rat', colloquial German for 'gambler' – note by the editor of Freud's work]). He would have found himself in a serious position if one of his comrades had not advanced him the amount. After he had left the army and become well off, he had tried to find this friend in need so as to pay him back the money, but had not managed to trace him. ... What the rat punishment stirred up more than anything else was his *anal erotism*, which had played an important part in his childhood and had been kept in activity for many years by a constant irritation due to worms. In this way rats came to have the meaning of '*money*'. The patient gave an indication of this connection by reacting to the word '*Ratten*' [Rats] with the association '*Raten*' ['instalments' – Ernst, like his father, also had to give back money]. But the patient was also familiar with the fact that rats are carriers of dangerous infectious diseases; he could therefore

employ them as symbols of his dread (justifiable enough in the army) of *syphilitic infection*. ... Again, in another sense, the penis itself is a carrier of syphilitic infection; and in this way he could consider the rat as a male organ of sex. ... A penis (especially a child's penis) can easily be compared to a *worm*, and the captain's story had been about rats burrowing in someone's anus, just as the large round-worms had in his when he was a child. ... All of this material, and more besides, was woven into the fabric of the rat discussion behind the screen-association *'heiraten'* ['to marry']. [Ernst was uncertain and put off the marriage with Gisela Adler (later on his wife)]

Rat-money-worm-anus-father-fiancée = Ernst is frightened of rats, and fears that something will happen to his father and his friend Gisela. What could happen to them? Rats are associated with children. Rats bite. Ernst remembers that when he was a child he bit someone, and his father punished him for this, but Mahony has demonstrated that there were no precise references to this recollection. But where did Ernst bite him? We return to Ernst's obsessive thought. The rat bites the anus. Anus = place where children think that sexual intercourse takes place. Therefore: I, Ernst, hide this thought in my unconscious: rat bites anus = Ernst penetrates the anus of his father and Gisela.

So far so good (in a manner of speaking), if you accept the methodology of free associations and their interpretation (we'll ignore here the philological correctness of some of Freud's interpretations, a subject that has been adequately examined by Sebastiano Timpanaro). However, Mahony demonstrates that the interpretation is based on factual elements that are either untrue or have been "adjusted". He does this by comparing Freud's notes (which were miraculously saved – a trick of the unconscious) and the account published by Freud in 1909. Mahony's conclusion is that

> through the alteration of temporal sequence, Freud's construction given to the Rat Man becomes in turn a fictionalised reconstruction shown to the reader. Obviously Freud thought that to have his construction refer to an episode he heard only later made for a better story.

Indeed Freud wants to show that he previously understood some interpretations that are then confirmed by episodes and events that the patient subsequently reveals. During the First World War, Lanzer was captured by the Russians and he died at thirty-six (in 1914). According to Freud, analysis had led "to the complete restoration of the patient's personality", but there is no evidence that his psyche was in fact freed of these obsessions. Indeed, it would appear from Freud's letter to Jung in 1909 that there were still some problems:

> The point that still gives him trouble (father-complex and transference) has shown up clearly in my conversations with this intelligent and grateful man.

Freud tested his abilities with the analysis of cases of which he had no direct experience. Thus in 1909 he published a fascinating account of the case of little Hans, basing himself on evidence provided by the child's father. In 1911, he published another famous essay on "Chairman Schreber", based on Schreber's own memoirs.

Little Hans was called Herbert Graf, and was the son of Max, a well known Austrian musicologist, and Olga König. The Graf family were a typical psycho-analytical constellation: Olga was under analysis with

Freud, and their son Herbert was analysed by his father who referred back to Sigmund. Indeed, Max frequented meetings of the Psychoanalytical Society, which were held at Freud's home on Wednesday evenings, and became an enthusiastic student of the subject. He analysed his wife Olga, and Freud was a frequent visitor to Graf's home. Herbert was frightened that a horse would bite him, and analysis of this phobia was used to construct the case of little Hans involving the fundamental elements of the Freudian theory of psychosexual development: episodes of masturbation, love for the mother and hatred of the father, fear of castration, etc. It has been noted by various writers who are unsympathetic to Freud's methodology that Herbert provides perfectly sensible explanations for his fears, but Freud and his father always take him down the path of new and peculiar interpretations. Freud advises the father to tell his son that

> all this business about horses was a piece of nonsense and nothing more. The truth was, his father was to say, that he was very fond of his mother and wanted to be taken into her bed. The reason he was afraid of horses now was that he had taken so much interest in their widdlers ...

But little Herbert repeats that his fear – the "nonsense" as the "Professor" (Sigmund Freud) calls it – is based on reality. Here is a crucial part of the dialogue between the thirty-five-year-old father (I) and the five-year-old son (Hans), where the father is not only his father but also his analyst:

> Hans: And I'm most afraid of furniture-vans, too.
> I: Why?
> Hans: I think when furniture-horses are dragging
>   a heavy van they'll fall down.

I: So you're not afraid with a small cart?

Hans: No. I'm not afraid with a small cart or with a post-office van. I'm most afraid too when a bus comes along.

I: Why? Because it's so big?

Hans: No. Because once a horse in a bus fell down.

I: When?

Hans: Once when I went out with Mummy in spite of my "nonsense", when I bought the waistcoat. (This was subsequently confirmed by his mother.)

I: What did you think when the horse fell down?

Hans: Now it'll always be like this. All horses in buses'll fall down.

I: In all buses?

Hans: Yes. And in furniture-vans too. Not often in furniture-vans.

At this stage the father poses the fundamental question for psychoanalytical theory, relating to the correspondence between reality and fantasy.

I: You had your nonsense already at that time?

Hans: No. I only got it then. When the horse in the bus fell down, it gave me such a fright, really! That was when I got the nonsense.

A few days before this conversation, father and son had visited Freud, who wrote:

But as I saw the two of them sitting in front of me and at the same time heard Hans's description of his anxiety-horses, a further piece of the solution shot through my mind, and a piece which I could well understand might escape his father. I asked Hans jokingly whether his horses wore eyeglasses, to which he replied that they did not. I then asked him whether his father wore eyeglasses, to which, against all the evidence, he once more said no. Finally I

> asked him whether by "the black round the mouth"
> he meant a moustache [Hans was particularly
> disturbed by what the horses had in front of their
> eyes and the blackness around their mouths].

Who knows, Hans was perhaps a little surprised when
he replied to those questions about horses with glasses
and moustaches, and he may have gone quiet. This is
how the "Professor" dealt with the situation and
explained what was really happening:

> And then I disclosed to him that he was afraid of his
> father, precisely because he was so fond of his
> mother. It must be, I told him, that he thought his
> father was angry with him on that account; but this
> was not so, his father was fond of him of spite of it,
> and he might admit everything to him without any
> fear. Long before he was in the world, I went on, I
> had known that a little Hans would come who would
> be so fond of his mother that he would be bound to
> feel afraid of his father because of it; and I told his
> father this.

This was how the fifty-five-year-old Sigmund Freud
helped Herbert Graf, barely five years old, to establish
a scientific view of the world. But Herbert is bewildered
by these questions about glasses and moustaches on
horses, and he can't quite understand why he is
supposed to be frightened of his dad because he loves
his mum. Herbert appears to be suggesting that this is
a very funny way to construct an argument. But Freud
explains that it is really a very simple argument. Do
you love your mummy? Well then, you hate your
daddy. That is why you laugh when I ask you whether
horses wear glasses and have moustaches. In other
words, are you frightened of horses that wear glasses
and have moustaches? Of course you are, because you
hate your father. And why do you hate your father?

Because you love your mummy. It could be considered a harmless play on words, if it weren't for the fact that there was a child involved, and that that child was being brought up by playing on his ingenuousness and on the persuasive powers of an adult professor. This was compounded by the use of what Freud called a "joking boastfulness" in order to influence the child: for some time Freud had been saying to Hans that before he came into the world, he had known that there would be a little Hans. While he was going down the stairs from Freud's flat, the redoubtable Herbert asked his father the following question:

> Does the Professor talk to God, as he can tell all that beforehand?

We do not know his father's reply. There are, in fact, other interesting details missing from Freud's account. For example, Freud does not tell us what he decided to buy Herbert on his third birthday (i.e. before any of the conversations just referred to), but we are told in the memoirs of the boy's father in 1942. What does the professor bring? Well, a lovely rocking horse, of course. A postscript, which Freud added to his report in 1922, reveals that Herbert visited him in Vienna. Thankfully, "Little Hans was now a strapping youth of nineteen. He declared that he was perfectly well, and suffered from no troubles or inhibitions." Herbert had read the "case of little Hans", and because of one detail, had guessed that he might have been the child who was frightened of horses.

Herbert became an eminent stage designer. He worked for the Metropolitan in New York and very often for Italian theatres, and ended up directing a theatre in Geneva. He was a friend of the greatest musicians in the twentieth century, and worked with Toscanini and Callas. It does not appear, however, that his love life was particularly happy. Even though Freud stated in the postscript that Herbert's "emotional life had successfully undergone one of the severest of ordeals" – the fact that his parents split up and then remarried was a source of anxiety. And so he needed to undergo further analysis.

There were other cases of protagonists discovering many years later that their "stories" had been written up. On other occasions, psychoanalysts have accidentally discovered that they were in the company of people described in Freud's case studies. Thus Ida Bauer came to know that she was the famous "clinical case of Dora" described by Sigmund Freud, when she underwent further analysis twenty years later with Felix Deutsch.

The same happened with another well known case described on this occasion by Melanie Klein: the case of Dick, a three-and-a-half-year-old child displaying psychotic symptoms. Klein's analysis started in 1929 and continued until 1941, when it was suspended until 1943, and finally ended in 1946. It was then taken up for a further three years with another analyst (totalling almost 17 years). Klein's biographer, Phyllis Grosskurth, met Dick when he was about fifty and the two read a few pages of Klein's article together. Dick agreed with some of Klein's notes (for example, the fact that he considered urine a dangerous substance), but disagreed with others (for example, that he saw a penis as an assault weapon). In the end Dick exclaimed: "If Melanie were alive today, I'd ring her and say 'Enough is enough'." Grosskurth was also able to find Richard, the protagonist of another famous case described by Klein in *Narrative of a Child Analysis* (published posthumously in 1961), when he was an adult. As a result of this meeting, Richard was to discover that he was the subject of an entire book. During the interview with Grosskurth, he recalled scenes from his analysis.

"Can you remember the first time you went to Mrs Klein, and what it was like? Would you describe it for me?"

"Oh, it's difficult to remember too much. I do recall the Girl Guide hut. There were two rooms, and there must have been a table. We must have had toys. The only toys I can remember were the battleships. I mentioned to you this morning that I remember going on about the fact that we were going to bomb the Germans, and seize Berlin, and so on and so on and then Brest. Melanie seized on b-r-e-a-s-t, which of course was very much her angle. She would often talk about the 'big Mummy genital' and the 'big Daddy genital', or the 'good Mummy genital' or the 'bad Daddy genital.' I can't remember what other things she had to say. It was very much a strong interest in genitalia."

"Was that right from the beginning?"

"Yes, very much so."

Richard only remembered having seen Klein once after the analysis, when he was about sixteen. Klein claimed to have seen Richard again on several occasions. The memories do not agree with each other, but Richard remembered Melanie with fondness:

When we met on a subsequent occasion, I brought along a copy of *Narrative of a Child Analysis*, which he had never seen before. He gazed at the photograph of Melanie Klein on the back cover. 'Dear old Melanie,' he murmured. Then he suddenly put the photograph to his lips and kissed it affectionately.

It is certainly curious that patients in clinical cases do not know that they are or will become the subjects of detailed accounts by their analysts. Klein was following the example of Jung, who spoke at the Amsterdam conference of a case of hysterical paranoia as if it were a specimen of organic pathology and not a person who might suffer from such a detached description from someone to whom she was emotionally attached. It is generally thought that the perception of patients as case studies, objects and non-persons was typical of the traditional nineteenth-century approach to psychiatry. But psychoanalysis also invites us to visit a freak show: "the Wolf Man", "the Rat Man", a "case of hysteria", a "case of obsessive neurosis", a "case of paranoia", and so on. These clinical portraits are hung in public galleries for all to admire. Their restorations and retouching are commented upon. Each has its own critical history and literature. The bibliography continues to swell. But who ever thinks of the models who posed for these portraits?

Of course, it will be argued that it is impossible to keep up with all your patients once therapy has been completed. But this will not stand up when it comes to paradigmatic cases used for building the theoretical and therapeutic models on which psychoanalysis is based. A doctor can prescribe a drug without having to verify its efficacy for every single patient, because this test has already been conducted on the first patients as a clinical trial. In the same way, a systematic verification of a therapy should have been conducted on the first clinical cases on which psychoanalysis was based ("the pillars on which psychoanalysis as an empirical science rests", as Kurt Eissler wrote), in order to corroborate the soundness of the theoretical principles.

The "case of Aimée" is one of the most disturbing cases of this indifference to the feelings of the analysed person, at least from what is shown by the published accounts. The protagonist of this story was Marguerite Pantaine. She was born in 1892 to a French middle-class family. Her mother suffered from persecution symptoms. Marguerite hoped to escape from the monotony of French provincial life, but managed only to obtain employment at the post office and to marry another clerk, René Anzieu. She started to develop twin psychological dimensions: the daily grind of family life (in the meantime her son Didier had been born) and a fantastic and delirious world. At some stage, she became convinced that she was being persecuted by Huguette Duflos, an actress who was famous at the time, and one day in 1931, she stabbed her. The actress survived and Marguerite ended up in Sainte-Anna Hospital, where she became the "case of Aimée".

Jacques Lacan was one of the staff at this renowned hospital, and his analytical antecedents went back to Sigmund Freud. He was to be analysed by Rudolph Loewenstein, who in turn analysed Hanns Sachs, a member of the secret committee and one of Freud's loyal followers. Equally loyal was Princesss Marie Bonaparte, who was analysed by Freud himself, and was for a time Loewenstein's lover. Lacan treated Marguerite and described the case in his medical thesis (entitled *Paranoid Psychosis and its Relation to Personality*, 1932), whose originality and profound argumentation made him famous. For his work, the French psychoanalyst used two novels that Marguerite had written and would have liked to publish. These were not returned in spite of her protestations. Lacan's diagnosis is terse and at times incomprehensible for the uninitiated. It adopts the style of clinical files produced in the nineteenth century, with plenty of photos of the patient:

> Paranoid psychosis. Recent delusions culminating in attempted homicide. Obsessions apparently resolved after the attack. Dreamlike state. Interpretations significant, extensive, and concentric and grouped around the overriding idea: threats to her son. Emotional preoccupation: her duty toward the latter. Polymorphic impulses provoked by anxiety: approaches to an author and to her future victim. Urgent need to write. Results sent to English royal family. Others of a polemic or bucolic nature. Caffeine dependency. Dietary deviations.

But, leaving aside this unfeeling catalogue of symptoms, who was Marguerite in her daily life? Elisabeth Roudinesco was very effective in her portrait of a woman divided in two:

> On the one hand there was the everyday world of her post office activities, in which she more or less adapted to reality. On the other hand she led an imaginary existence made up of dreams and delusions. On the Right Bank, Marguerite worked in the central post office in the rue du Louvre; on the Left Bank she lived in the Hôtel de la Nouvelle France in the rue Saint-André-des-Arts. As soon as she left her place of work she became an intellectual, taking private lessons, haunting libraries, addicted to coffee. But despite all her efforts she failed one professional examination and in three attempts at the *baccalauréat*.

Roudinesco has demonstrated that the way Lacan created this case study "was closer to his own theoretical preoccupations than to Marguerite Pantaine's true situation." Without denying that Marguerite was clearly a disturbed person, it has to be said that Lacan's portrait does not faithfully reflect the real clinical data. Lacan, writes Roudinesco, "modified certain events in her story to such an extent that it is still difficult even now to distinguish between intentional distortions and genuine mistakes." At that time Lacan had not yet started his analysis with Loewenstein, so it was not possible – as he himself pointed out – to provide Marguerite with psychoanalytical therapy, even though he interpreted the case through a psychoanalytical approach. This is what the son Didier wrote about his mother's therapy:

> When he examined her in the course of a series of interviews, Lacan was not yet trained as a psychoanalyst and made no attempt at psycho-therapy, a kind of treatment that in any case she would have refused: she often told my wife and myself that she found Lacan too attractive and too much of a clown to be trusted.

In 1949 Lacan started to analyse Didier, without knowing that he was the son of the person who had made him famous, or to be more precise and using the words of Roudinesco, "we know that in 1949 the name Anzieu couldn't really have been unknown to Lacan. But he had repressed the knowledge and didn't want to admit as much to Marguerite's son." Didier, who in turn became an eminent psychoanalyst, did not know that his analyst had in the past analysed his mother. In the meantime, poor Marguerite had become the cook of Alfred Lacan, Jacques's father (Fig. 5), so she was able to see Jacques on several occasions. In the end, Didier found out from his mother that she was the protagonist in the case of Aimée. Didier rushed off to the library to get hold of the work on his mother by his own psychoanalyst and read the clinical "history" for the first time. He then clashed with Jacques, who was guilty of having created this intrigue between analyst and patients (mother and son), but the great man shrugged off the criticism, claiming that he had not realised straightaway. All this was happening while Marguerite continued to complain that Lacan had treated her as a madwoman and, what is more, as a text-book example of "erotomania".

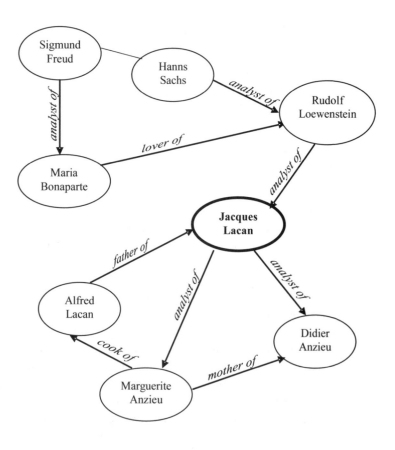

Fig 5. The constellation for Jacques Lacan

According to Roudinesco's investigations, Marguerite's granddaughter Christine Anzieu noted some significant features in her grandmother's personality:

> Like her parents, Christine knew about the past, and far from denying Marguerite's madness she saw traces of it in many of her attitudes. But she never felt she was face to face with such an organised paranoia as Lacan had described. She sensed the persecution, the passion, the mysticism, the desire to better herself, the violence, but what struck her most was an extraordinary capacity for love. And Marguerite was interested in knowledge of all kinds, ranging from physics to Hinduism and including the Breton language. She wanted to learn everything, know everything, read everything.

But once Marguerite Pantaine Anzieu had become a "case", she was condemned to remain one for the rest of her life. She was and had to be the prototype of paranoid psychosis, irrespective of whether or not she had been cured. For Lacan she only existed as the "case of Aimée". His father's cook and his patient's mother was unquestionably another woman. It sounds like an invented story, a film perhaps, but the documents produced by Roudinesco in her magnificent biography of Lacan demonstrate that psychoanalytical reality far exceeds psychoanalytical fantasy.

Chapter 5
The true story of the "Wolf Man"

In a letter dated 8 February 1910, Freud wrote to Ferenczi that he had started to treat "a new patient from Odessa, a very rich Russian with compulsive feelings". The analysis lasted four years and was the occasion for the publication in 1918 of one of Freud's best known cases – that of the Wolf Man. Jones, in his biography of the founding father of psychoanalysis, defined this case as "assuredly the best of the series. Freud was then at the very height of his powers, a confident master of his method."

Freud provided not only a detailed description of the genesis of his patient's psychological disorders, but also a model of therapeutic treatment. As Freud repeated many times, psychoanalysis was not only a theory of the psyche, but also a therapeutic proposal, and it was precisely through the success of its therapy that psychoanalytical theory would prove its worth. But was the Wolf Man cured of his neurosis after the first analysis with Freud and the second one with Ruth Mack Brunswick?

Yes he was, according to Freud: "I parted from him, regarding him as cured, a few weeks before the unexpected outbreak of the Great War". According to Ruth Mack Brunswick, the answer was also yes: "The therapeutic results were excellent." Another affirmative answer came from Muriel Gardiner, a psychoanalyst who had been analysed by Freud. She was the confidante and protectress of the Wolf Man:

Thanks to his analysis, the Wolf Man was able to survive shock after shock and stress after stress – with suffering, it is true, but with more strength and resilience than one might expect. The Wolf Man himself is convinced that without psychoanalysis he would have been condemned to lifelong misery. ... There can be no doubt that Freud's analysis saved the Wolf Man from a crippled existence, and Dr Brunswick's reanalysis overcame a serious acute crisis, both enabling the Wolf Man to lead a long and tolerably healthy life.

The clerical worker Sergey Konstantinovich Pankeyev, who was identified as the Wolf Man by the Viennese journalist Karin Obholzer in 1973, was not of the same opinion. Sergey Konstantinovich, born in 1887, lived a long life (dying in 1979) and was able to say his bit about what it was like to be the "patient from Odessa". He spoke to Obholzer "confidentially":

> Pankeyev: Instead of doing me some good, psychoanalysts did me harm. ... In reality, the whole thing looks like a catastrophe. I am in the same state as when I first came to Freud, and Freud is no more.
>
> Obholzer: Do you believe that Freud could help you today?
>
> Pankeyev: No, I don't believe that.

Sergey Konstantinovich was not only angry with Freud, but with all the psychoanalysts, psychiatrists and psychotherapists who had treated him without achieving very much. Fear and depression had been present throughout his life, with high and lows. "The chief feature," Gardiner wrote, "is the prominence of his obsessional doubting, brooding, questioning, his being completely engrossed in his own problems and unable to relate to others, unable to read or to paint."

But what was Sergey Konstantinovich's comment on this lack of contact with the outside world? "That's all false too. Contact was never lost. On the contrary, contact with others was too close, everything turned into conflict. It's all false."

Before and after the analysis with Freud, Sergey Konstantinovich was treated by a stream of psychiatrists and psychotherapists. As the son of a very wealthy landowner, he was able to go round various European clinics and consult the luminaries of the period. Hence he was treated in St Petersburg by Vladimir M. Bechterev, the most authoritative Russian psychiatrist, in Munich by Emil Kraepelin, the leading exponent of traditional academic psychiatry, and in Berlin by Theodor Ziehen, another leading German psychiatrist. The treatments were typical of psychiatry of the time: hypnosis, physical therapies like baths, massages, etc. He then turned to psychotherapy: after a brief treatment with Leonid Drosnez in Odessa, he started psychoanalytical therapy with Freud in Vienna, which lasted from 1910 to 1914, and then from 1919 to 1920. He was also treated by Moshe Wulff, one of the leading exponents of psychoanalysis in Russia. Then it was the turn of Ruth Mack Brunswick in Vienna from 1926 to 1927. Other analysts with whom Sergey Konstantinovich underwent more or less systematic therapeutic treatments were subsequently Frederick S. Weil, Kurt Eissler, Wilhelm Solms-Rödelheim and Muriel Gardiner.

In particular Sergey Konstantinovich had very little liking for Eissler, the loyal custodian of the Freud Archive at the Library of Congress in Washington. On the other hand, Eissler would fly every year from America to Europe to visit him and continue the analysis, even in the final years of the Wolf Man's life. Sergey Konstantinovich told Obholzer in the interview

130

that Eissler did not realise that things had changed and that he could not continue to talk to an elderly man of over seventy years about "psychoanalytic symbols like castration fear and God knows what else". He added that Eissler was "a terrible *simplificateur*, he simplifies everything."

It should be noted that Sergey Konstantinovich was a frequent visitor to doctors' surgeries for a variety of illnesses, ranging from blennorrhoea at the age of eighteen to nasal complaints and repeated dental problems. By one of those quirks of fate, Sergey encountered more than one "wolf" during his lifetime: Wolf (which means the same in German) was the name of two of his doctors, and one of his Russian psychoanalysts was called Wulff (a westernised version of the surname Vul'f), which inevitably recalled the wide open mouth illustrated in an edition of *Little Red Riding-Hood* that his little sister Anna used to show him in order to frighten him. Lastly there was a strict Wolf, his Latin teacher.

However, the Wolf Man got his name from a dream that he described to Freud during analysis:

> I dreamt that it was night and that I was lying in my bed. (My bed stood with its foot towards the window; in front of the window there was a row of old walnut trees. I know it was winter when I had the dream, and night-time.) Suddenly the window opened of its own accord, and I was terrified to see that some white wolves were sitting on the big walnut tree in front of the window. There were six or seven of them. The wolves were quite white, and looked more like foxes or sheep-dogs, for they had big tails like foxes and they had their ears pricked like dogs when they pay attention to something. In great terror, evidently of being eaten up by the wolves, I screamed and woke up.

The dream went back to a period in which Sergey Konstantinovich was four, but it masked an episode that occurred when he was one and a half. According to Freud, Sergey Konstantinovich had seen something that only later would he be able to understand, and this understanding had been worked out from the dream. Sergey Konstantinovich, Freud explained, had been in his parents' bedroom:

> He had been sleeping in his cot, then, in his parents' bedroom, and woke up, perhaps because of his rising fever, in the afternoon, possibly at five o'clock, the hour which was later marked out by depression. It harmonises with our assumption that it was a hot summer's day, if we suppose that his parents had retired, half undressed [in white underclothes: the *white* wolves – Freud's note], for an afternoon *siesta*. When he woke up, he witnessed a coitus *a tergo* [from behind], three times repeated; he was able to see his mother's genitals as well as his father's organ; and he understood the process as well as its significance.

According to Freud's reconstruction of the facts, this scene gave rise to little Sergey Konstantinovich's neurosis, a collection of behaviour patterns character-ised by phobias for animals and by religious rituals:

> Thus he could recollect how he had suffered from a fear, which his sister exploited for the purpose of tormenting him. There was a particular picture-book, in which a wolf was represented, standing upright and striding along. Whenever he caught sight of this picture he began to scream like a lunatic that he was afraid of the wolf coming and eating him up. His sister, however, always succeeded in arranging things so that he was obliged to see this picture, and was delighted at his terror. Meanwhile he was also frightened of other animals as well, big and little.

Once he was running after a beautiful big butterfly, with striped yellow wings which ended in points, in the hope of catching it. (It was no doubt a 'swallow-tail'.) He was suddenly seized with a terrible fear of the creature, and, screaming, gave up the chase. He also felt fear and loathing of beetles and caterpillars. Yet he could also remember that at this very time he used to torment beetles and cut caterpillars to pieces. Horses, too, gave him an uncanny feeling. If a horse was beaten he began to scream, and he was once obliged to leave a circus on that account. On other occasions he himself enjoyed beating horses. ...

He related how during a long period he was very pious. Before he went to sleep he was obliged to pray for a long time and to make an endless series of signs of the cross. In the evening, too, he used to make the round of all the holy pictures that hung in the room, taking a chair with him, upon which he climbed, and used to kiss each one of them devoutly. It was utterly inconsistent with this pious ceremonial – or, on the other hand, perhaps it was quite consistent with it – that he should recollect some blasphemous thoughts which used to come into his head like an inspiration from the devil. He was obliged to think 'God-swine' or 'God-shit'. Once while he was on a journey to a health resort in Germany he was tormented by the obsession of having to think of the Holy Trinity whenever he saw three heaps of horse-dung or other excrement lying in the road.

All this happened because he had once seen his father penetrate his mother from behind. However, there have been many queries about this interpretation. Sergey Konstantinovich's own assertion would probably suffice:

The whole thing is improbable because in Russia, children sleep in the nanny's bedroom, not in their parents'. It's possible, of course, that there was an exception, how do I know? But I have never been able to remember anything of that sort.

Everything is therefore down to Freud's interpretation, about which Sergey Konstantinovich has some simple but interesting things to say:

> In my story, what was explained by dreams? Nothing, as far as I can see. Freud traces everything back to the primal scene which he derives from the dream. But the scene does not occur in the dream. When he interprets the white wolves as nightshirts or something like that, for example, linen sheets or clothes, that's somehow far-fetched, I think. That scene in the dream where the windows open and so on and the wolves are sitting there, and his interpretation, I don't know, those things are miles apart. It's terribly far-fetched ..., that primal scene is no more than a construct.

At this stage some analyst could abruptly interrupt: hold on, we need to be wary of patients' retrospective interpretations, although they can be useful for the purposes of understanding their resistances and transference. So Obholzer challenged Sergey Konstantinovich by saying: "Your resistance up to the present day is so strong that you don't want to remember." Sergey Konstantinovich responded with an assertion worthy of theoretical scientific reasoning: "Well, that would also be a supposition, wouldn't it? But it is no proof."

Let us now move on to another celebrated interpretation of the wolf dream put forward by Otto Rank, another psychoanalyst, albeit a heretical one, and then we will take a critical look at some considerations developed by historians of psychoanalysis. According to Rank, the wolves represent the members of the "Secret Committee" founded in Vienna in 1912 to safeguard the psychoanalytical movement. Sergey Konstantinovich could have seen the first members of the Committee (Ernest Jones, Karl Abraham, Hanns Sachs, Otto Rank, Sandor Ferenczi and Anton von Freund) at Freud's home, and then dreamt about them. He could have seen their photographs hanging in Freud's study while he was lying on the couch or perhaps, we could add, he saw some of them while he was in the waiting room. Perhaps he was frightened, and that fear took on the guise of wolves (white ones, like doctors in white coats).

Mahony, on the other hand, finds the sexual prowess of Sergey Konstantinovich's father completely fantastic: he claims that sexual intercourse three times in half an hour would be worthy of a "super-macho" capable of putting the legendary heroes of *Playboy* to shame. But what does "three times" mean? Three penetrations of the penis in the vagina, with a final ejaculation? Or three penetrations, each followed by an ejaculation? Could little Sergey Konstantinovich have understood the difference? Then, Mahony points out, during sexual intercourse "from behind", it is not easy to see the genitals of the two partners. How could a feverish child have seen that the mother did not have a penis (the image that was supposed to have caused his future castration complex)? Fabiano Bassi, who has critically analysed the whole question, has observed:

> We suddenly collide with a wall that common sense and logic prevent us from going beyond. I very much doubt in fact that it would be easy to find someone willing to believe that a child of a year and a half, suffering from an attack of malarial fever, could have the strength to act as a spectator for half an hour without being noticed, and be capable of drawing the right conclusions about what was happening, namely

that there were two people having sexual intercourse precisely three times (can the meaning of three be understood by a child of eighteen months?).

In truth, Freud himself must have had a few doubts, because at a certain point in his treatise, he wonders whether the child actually witnessed the sexual intercourse between his parents: "I should myself be glad to know whether the primal scene in my present patient's case was a fantasy or a real experience". But a few pages later, Freud adds that "it is also a matter of indifference in this connection whether we choose to regard it as a primal *scene* or as a primal *fantasy*". Indeed, a little earlier, he had stated that the question was closed and irrelevant: "I intend on this occasion to close the discussion of the reality of the primal scene with a *non liquet*" ("the question is not clear", the formula used by the ancient Roman judges when they suspended a sentence).

In the eyes of psychoanalysts, however, that scene has conserved all its significance for understanding and interpreting the behaviour of Sergey Konstantinovich, particularly in the sexual field. Having seen his parents united in sexual intercourse from behind, he became fixated on that position ("the man upright, and the woman bent down like an animal," Freud writes), and, at the right moment, he is supposed to have penetrated women from behind. Freud reports that, since Sergey Konstantinovich was small, he had been aroused by the sight of maids or peasant women washing the floor on their knees, because every time this recalled the "primal scene" of his father and mother. Concerning the episode in which Sergey Konstantinovich is supposed to have urinated while watching his nanny Grusha, Freud had this to say:

When he saw the girl on the floor engaged in scrubbing it, and kneeling down, with her buttocks projecting and her back horizontal, he was faced once again with the posture which his mother had assumed in the copulation scene. She became his mother to him; he was seized with sexual excitement owing to the activation of this picture; and, like his father (whose action he can only have regarded at the time as micturition), he behaved in a masculine way towards her.

This fixation with the position not agreeable to "missionaries" (who, as is well known, introduced the "good savages" to face-to-face sexual intercourse, which is more spiritual than the bestial intercourse from behind) also affected his relations with his wife Teresa. When questioned by Obholzer on this point, Sergey Konstantinovich replied that Freud's assertion was "incorrect", indeed "during our first coitus she sat on top of me." Similarly, Mack Brunswick's assertions concerning his sexual habits ("he now frequently accompanied prostitutes to their lodging where, on account of his fear of venereal disease, his relations with them were limited to masturbation in their presence") were for Sergey Konstantinovich nothing more than the psychoanalyst's fantasies. This including her assertion that he only masturbated at the time of important holidays:

> Pankeyev: I have no idea what that is supposed to mean.
> Obholzer: But that's what she [Mack Brunswick] writes.
> Pankeyev: That I said that?
> Obholzer: Yes, "Of course, I only masturbated on the big holidays."
> Pankeyev: No such thing. That would be stupid. What does that have to do with holidays?

> Obholzer: She [Mack Brunswick] writes that you felt a special way about holidays.
>
> Pankeyev: Well, she was fantasising. There's no such thing, what silliness. Mack also invented things occasionally.

Clearly not imagining that one day Sergey Konstantinovich Pankeyev would be interviewed, Mack Brunswick (and others) must have thought it possible to add a little colour to their accounts by inventing at least a few details, but one detail alone could reveal a whole personality.

The other significant denial by Sergey Konstantinovich concerned Ernest Jones. Freud's official biographer claimed to have entered into a correspondence with the Wolf Man. However much Obholzer urged him to search his memory, Sergey Konstantinovich replied repeatedly and very definitely that he had never heard any mention of Jones: "He [Jones] writes that I corresponded with him. I never corresponded with him." Another not insignificant problem for historians of psychoanalysis concerns the first meeting between Sergey Konstantinovich and Freud. In his biography of Freud, Jones wrote that the Wolf Man "initiated the first hour of treatment with the offer to have rectal intercourse with Freud and then to defecate on his head." Jones referred to a letter of 13 February 1910 to Ferenczi in which Freud described the episode in the following manner: "A rich young Russian, whom I took on because of compulsive tendencies, admitted the following transferences to me after the first session: Jewish swindler, he would like to use me from behind and shit on my head."

Therefore it was Sergey Konstantinovich who feared that Freud wanted anal sex with him (and most probably only in the metaphorical sense of cheating him), but in reality (that is psychoanalytical reality) it was him who wanted anal sex with Freud. Sergey Konstantinovich was astounded when he read for the first time this passage from Jones's book which Obholzer had bought him. He denied that this episode ever took place.

On the question of "from behind" and "in front", he only remembered what Freud had explained to him: he had got into the habit of turning his back to his patients (in this sense, he was presenting his "behind" to them) while sitting at the top of the couch. He had started to do this after an attempted seduction by one of his young female patients (Freud had been seated at the bottom of the couch and the patient "did some sort of gymnastics with her feet and lifted her skirt"). He remembered that he too had turned over on the couch, but to assert that this amounted to a request for anal sex seemed to him to be complete folly: "Those are delusions... People fantasise."

The photos of Sergey Konstantinovich show him to have always been sad and disconsolate – as a child, as a young adult, and as a mature man, while he walked along the streets of Vienna in a long dark coat, with a scarf and a narrow-rimmed hat, his eyes fixed on the ground. What kind of life did the Wolf Man have? A difficult life in itself, leaving aside the phobias about wolves, the sexual difficulties, the aesthetic obsessions about his nose, and the continuous dental treatment (he had a good tooth extracted in place of the bad one – far from having a castration complex).

Above all, his was an unfortunate family in terms of psychological disorders and tragic deaths. The father, who suffered from a serious form of depression, was treated by Kraepelin, ended up in psychiatric clinics on several occasions and committed suicide at forty-nine with an overdose of sleeping tablets. His paternal grandmother also committed suicide, as a result of depression following the death of her only daughter who was struck down by scarlet fever at the age of eight. Not to mention Anna, Sergey Konstantinovich's sister, who used poison to commit suicide at twenty. His paternal uncle, who suffered from a serious form of paranoia, was treated in a psychiatric clinic by Professor Sergey Korsakov, a famous Russian psychiatrist and neurologist (known for the alcoholism syndrome that carries his name). As Sergey Konstantinovich recalled, this uncle died completely mad in total solitude at his home in Crimea: "It was said that cows, pigs, and other domestic animals were the only company he tolerated and permitted to share his living quarters. It was easy to imagine what these quarters must have looked like." Lastly, a cousin on his mother's side also ended up in a psychiatric hospital.

Sergey Konstantinovich's life was not only marked by these tragic events in his family. He was equally unfortunate in his romantic life. This was Sergey Konstantinovich's account of his first meeting with Teresa Keller, a nurse at the psychiatric clinic close to Munich where he was treated:

> It was carnival time, and on the evening of the day I moved into the sanatorium a fancy dress ball for the staff and the nurses was to take place. Dr. H. and I were also invited to this ball. Watching the dancers I was immediately struck by an extra-ordinarily beautiful woman. She was perhaps in her middle or late twenties and thus a few years older than myself. ... Her blue-black hair was parted in the middle, and her features were of such regularity and delicacy that they might have been chiselled by a sculptor. She was dressed as a Turkish woman, and since she was a definitely southern type with

somewhat oriental characteristics, this costume suited her very well and could hardly have been better chosen. The other dancers looked frolicsome and sometimes clownish, but she kept her serious expression the whole time. Although it contrasted with the gaiety of the others, it did not seem at all out of place. I was so fascinated by this woman that I kept wondering how this apparition from *The Arabian Nights* could ever have become one of the people employed in a Bavarian sanatorium.

Having overcome his family's opposition (Teresa was divorced and had a daughter), the two got married and constantly moved from one city to another, living modestly in Odessa, Moscow and Vienna. Following the October Revolution, Sergey Konstantinovich had lost most of his assets, and had to put up with working as a clerk in an insurance company in Vienna. Then came yet another suicide:

The month of March was drawing to a close, and the last day of this month, March 31, 1938, was to be for me the most disastrous day of my whole life. For it was on this day that something happened which I had never believed possible: while I was at the office, Teresa did actually turn on the gas. ... When I came home on this day of misery, I saw to my surprise the old servant, who helped Teresa in the household two or three times a week, walking up and down before the door of our apartment. To my question what she was doing there, I received the strange reply: "Your wife asked me to come to look after you."

Now I knew that there was madness at work ... I stormed into our hallway where warning notes had been put up: "Don't turn on the light – danger of gas." From there I rushed into the kitchen, which was filled with the streaming gas as with a thick fog. Teresa was sitting near the gas jet, bent over the kitchen table, on which lay several letters of farewell.

> This sight was so terrible that I simply cannot describe it.

Was this spectacle reality, a dream or a fantasy? This time no one asked the question. No one had the courage to ask Sergey Konstantinovich whether he had had a bad dream when he repeated, "Why did this have to happen to me? Why did my wife kill herself?" Reality, dream or fantasy hardly matter in this context – Freud would have said *non liquet*.

A more understanding attitude towards Sergey Konstantinovich can be found in the memoirs of Muriel Gardiner, the very wealthy American psychoanalyst who helped several colleagues through the difficult times of Nazism, and funded a nursery school with a psychoanalytical slant in London and the foundation of the Freud Museum. Gardiner was also generous to Sergey Konstantinovich, although she did not encourage his desire to move to the United States, very probably because of her fears that he could end up amongst psychoanalysis's detractors. To understand the personality of this analyst, who was a socialist and anti-Nazi activist and assisted in the illegal immigration of numerous party members and Jews, one can do no better than read the wonderful portrait of her provided by the writer Lillian Hellman in her book *Pentimento: A Book of Portraits* (1973). In the novel, Muriel takes the name of Julia, the same Julia who is played by Vanessa Redgrave in the film *Julia* by Fred Zinnemann, while Lillian is played by Jane Fonda. Lillian tells the story:

> I knew, for example, that she had become, maybe always was, a Socialist, and lived by her principles, in a one-room apartment in a slum district of Vienna, sharing her great fortune with whoever needed it. She allowed herself very little, wanted very

little. Oddly, gifts to me did not come into the denial: they were many and extravagant. Through the years, whenever she saw anything I might like, it was sent to me: old Wedgwood pieces, a Toulouse-Lautrec drawing, a fur-lined coat we saw together in Paris, a set of Balzac that she put in a rare Empire desk, and a wonderful set of Georgian jewellery.

Gardiner, in her autobiography of 1983, denies ever having known Hellman, and still less having been her friend. But, in spite of the climate of dreams and fantasies to which we have been introduced, with invented stories and clinical cases, I still like to think of Muriel, as played by Vanessa Redgrave, meeting Sergey Konstantinovich in Vienna:

> I had known the Wolf Man in a distant sort of way for a number of years following the completion of his analysis by Ruth Mack Brunswick. At first he and I had drunk tea together every Wednesday afternoon while he patiently tried to teach me Russian. At these meetings, after devoting a conscientious hour to Russian grammar, we would relax and talk about more interesting things: Dostoyevsky, Freud, or the French Impressionists. He knew few people with whom he could talk about these beloved subjects, and I always enjoyed and profited by his acute observations which grew out of a really deep understanding of human nature, art, and psycho-analysis.

A subtle thread joins two famous Freudian cases: the Wolf Man and Dora. Gardiner was a confidante of Sergey Konstantinovich, and she encouraged him in his difficult life and helped him financially. However, Gardiner also became the wife of Joseph Buttinger, the leader of the Austrian Social-Democrats, and came into contact with other leading figures in the party such as Otto Bauer. Otto was the brother of Ida Bauer, the Dora of the famous Freudian case history!

In the articles and books on the Wolf Man, and in the memoirs of this Russian gentleman fallen on bad times, there are many references to historical events, doctors and famous people between the world wars. Thus Sergey Konstantinovich, the archetypal phobic and neurotic straight out of a psychoanalytical textbook, is in fact one of the minor heroes of Central Europe which, having left behind the Austro-Hungarian Empire, was moving towards the Nazi catastrophe. He was also a typical product of a Russia traumatised by civil war and drifting towards Stalinist repression.

Obholzer wrote of Sergey Konstantinovich: "When I came to know him, he struck me as a character invented by Schnitzler, an Art Nouveau personality. Sometimes when I thought of him, I felt he was the kind of man to whom one gave orchids." The reference to Art Nouveau is well chosen and quite suggestive. It is quite probable that, while he was being treated by the psychoanalyst Wulff, Sergey Konstantinovich went to the "Ryabusinsky House" in Moscow. This splendid little villa, considered the masterpiece of Russian Art Nouveau, was the headquarters of the Russian Society of Psychoanalysis and psychoanalytical nursery school, before becoming the home of the writer Maxim Gorky. Who knows if he did not meet Sabina Spielrein on the splendid and twisting marble staircae from the ground to the first floor? She, like Wulff, was a member of the society. He may equally have met Vasily, Stalin's son, who was educated to sexuality in accordance with the principles of psychoanalysis, like so many other members of the party's nomenklatura.

Aleksandr Etkind, in his book on the history of Russian psychoanalysis (1994), recalled the poetry of

Osip Mandelshtam, the Russian poet who died on his way to the gulags in the thirties, and wondered whether these lines written in 1908 were known to Sergey Konstantinovich and whether their disturbing image re-emerged during the analysis with Freud, which started two years later:

> In the wood there are Christmas trees
> with golden tinsel blazing
> in the thickets toy wolves are gazing
> with terrifying eyes.
>
> My fateful, foreboding sadness,
> my freedom, calm and silent,
> and you, always laughing, there, crystal
> of the inanimate sky-blue canopy!

Those figurines of wolves with their "frightening looks" hanging from the Christmas tree closely resemble the wolves that Sergey Konstantinovich drew to illustrate his dream better to Freud.

Let us go back to the Wolf Man, to Freud's typical example of "infantile neurosis", a paradigmatic case that an endless stream of psychoanalysts have practised on in order to learn the genesis of this disorder. But do we really believe that Sergey Konstantinovich suffered from a neurotic disorder? It would appear not. Many scholars have expressed their uncertainties and have been inclined to believe that the famous Russian patient suffered from some form of psychosis, ranging widely from from manic-depressive psychosis (Kraepelin's original diagnosis) to schizophrenia (Ludwig Binswanger's diagnosis). Ruth Mack Brunswick diagnosed "paranoia" and other contemporary psychoanalysts perceive Sergey Konstantinovich as a psychotic, paranoid or borderline patient. However, Sergey Konstantinovich still remains the Wolf Man, a prototype on which to exercise clinical interpretation, while the real person fades into nothing, hidden as usual behind the screen of psycho-analytical narration.

In July 1977 Sergey Konstantinovich Pankeyev was taken to a psychiatric hospital in Vienna following a breakdown. When Obholzer went to see him, she found him in a bare whitewashed little room with bars on the window and a door without a handle. The Wolf Man had ended up in a mental hospital, and he was to die there two years later.

During the journalist's first visit, Sergey Konstantinovich said to her: "Do you remember Goncharov's *Oblomov*? Then you know that the book is about a man who lies in bed all day long and dreams, dreams, dreams."

In the end, Sergey Konstantinovich was reconciled with his childhood fantasies of being about to fall into the clutches of some wolves:

> It was winter, and when darkness fell I sometimes went to a room where I would be undisturbed and where I thought nobody would hear me, and began to improvise. I imagined a lonely winter landscape with a sleigh drawn by a horse toiling through the snow. I tried to produce the sounds on my accordion which would match the mood of this fantasy.

Chapter 6
The case of George G:
a typical blunder

On the evening of 9 July 1938, George Gershwin, the great American musician and composer of *Rhapsody in Blue* and *Porgy and Bess*, was taken in a coma to the Cedars of Lebanon Hospital, Los Angeles. Emergency surgery on his brain revealed a tumour in the temporal lobe of his right hemisphere. The operation lasted four hours, but proved ineffectual. Gershwin died two days later, at eleven in the morning. He had not even reached his fortieth year.

In spite of being successful, extremely rich and very attractive to women, Gershwin was also insecure and constantly in search of something, almost as though he could never completely achieve his goal. Since adolescence, he had suffered from melancholia and depression. His mother, Rose, was always expressing her dissatisfaction with George's career, and was always ready to draw his attention to bad reviews of his music. Being possessive, she always managed to persuade him not to marry. At the same time she was cold and detached: if George as a child tried to kiss her, she would turn away. In Joan Peyser's biography, it is claimed that when George came under the neurosurgeons' scalpel, his brother Ira informed their mother so that she could catch the next plane and visit the hospital. But Rose was playing poker and replied that she didn't see what possible use her presence could serve.

For his part Gershwin did all he could to maintain a negative dependency on women by finding aggressive companions and establishing unstable romantic attachments. Then there were the recurring headaches: for his friends they were his strategy for attracting the attention of others, given his sense of loneliness and being neglected. There was even talk of a "Goldwin phobia", as musical circles defined it: Gershwin could not stand Goldwin, his producer, because he was a dull man who knew nothing of music. All this was supposed to cause the depression and headaches.

In 1937, a year before his death, George fell in love with the beautiful Paulette Goddard, the wife of Charlie Chaplin, and he started to visit her regularly, but the headaches got worse. On this point, Peyser refers to the view expressed by Anita Loos, a friend of Gershwin's:

> But George was not at all well. He was beset by headaches of alarming intensity. At that time Freud's psychoanalysis had come into vogue, bruited about by the people who understood it least. Among the first to be enticed by Freudian theories were George's kin. So they sent him to a Hollywood analyst who theorised that George's headaches were caused by his guilty love for the wife of a friend, Charlie Chaplin.

The pain was terrible and George said that it felt like a horse was biting his head. He bought a kind of helmet designed to prevent hair loss, but he used it for another purpose: by tightening it around his head, he was able to get some temporary relief. This helmet, which is reproduced in Peyser's biography, was equipped with a kind of crank that was turned above the head and strangely reminds you of the medieval helmets used for drilling the skull and extracting the "stone" of folly. Apart from the headaches, there were many other signs that something was not quite right with George's brain. Almost his entire behaviour should have alerted the suspicions of his relations and those who treated him with a psychoanalytical technique (the *talk cure*, as Anna O. called it). Particularly after 1934, George's condition worsened, and in early 1937 there were unambiguous signs of neurological disorders. He had slipped from the podium during recitals and the following evening his direction of music he had written himself was awkward. He suffered from a total intolerance of light (he would sit in his ostentatious house in Beverly Hills for hours in the dark with the curtains drawn). He had olfactory hallucinations (he often smelt burnt rubber) and sudden losses of consciousness. In his biography of the musician, Edward Jablonsky states:

> On one occasion, he suffered a dizzy spell while leaving the Brown Derby restaurant and fell to the sidewalk. One member of the party was not impressed. "Leave him there", she snapped, "all he wants is attention." ... There were periods of impaired co-ordination; his playing was poor; he dropped utensils on the table; he spilled water; he fell on the stairs. These inexplicable occurrences upset his sister-in-law. Once, after spilling food, he was asked to leave the table. Ira helped him upstairs to his room.

In the meantime, the psychoanalyst Gregory Zilboorg was dredging through George's unconscious without the least suspicion that there was something wrong in his head, apart from the problematic relationship with his mother. George was in analysis with Zilboorg from the spring of 1934 until autumn 1935. If accusations made by some of his patients hadn't dragged his name through the newspapers, Zilboorg would mainly have been remembered for his *History of Dynamic Psychiatry*. Known amongst the rich and sophisticated circles of New York as an eccentric psychoanalyst and enchanting showman, Zilboorg had had a fascinating past. This Russian Jew had been a member of Kerensky's government immediately after the 1917 Revolution until the Bolsheviks took power, and he had then emigrated to the United States. He boasted a Cordon Bleu diploma, and liked to display his incredible skills as a linguist. He could speak eight languages fluently.

Somebody of Gershwin's standing would be expected to use one of the more expensive and sought-after psychoanalysts in Manhattan. His fees were exorbitant: as much as one hundred dollars per session in the thirties. The analysis did not last long however, due to disagreements that arose between the patient and analyst during a month-long holiday in Mexico. In their company was another patient of Zilboorg's, Edward Warburg – so much for the rule that patients should not meet up with their analysts outside their place of work. Zilboorg's unorthodox relationship with Gershwin was examined by a commission of the Psychoanalytical Society of New York, when he was accused by another patient of demanding an extra thousand dollars a month for advice that he was providing on matters concerning work. How did Zilboorg react to the threat of expulsion from the Psychoanalytical Society? He threatened to sue anyone who voted against him, and suggested he might call as his defence patients of his colleagues who could reveal embarrassing information about them. So it all came to nothing, much to the relief of other leading psychoanalysts in New York.

Kay Swift, another of George's beautiful lovers as well as his assistant, and her husband James Paul Warburg were the ones who advised George to undergo analysis with Zilboorg. The husband and wife were already being treated by Zilboorg, who also had as a patient Paul's cousin Edward Warburg (Edward, the director of the American Ballet School, was so fond of Zilboorg that he continued analysis with him for twenty-six years). There is still one element missing to round off Gershwin's network. By now, the reader will know the picture well enough to wonder about the relationship between Gregory Zilboorg and Kay Swift – between the psychoanalyst and his patient? Peyser provides an answer:

> Katharine Weber says her grandmother, Kay Swift, told her that during the last eight months of her year-and-a-half treatment with Zilboorg, he engaged in sexual intercourse with her. Weber emphasises that this was not a romantic liaison; the sex took place during the sessions at the patient's expense [in every sense, we might add]. Weber quotes Swift: "He was the only man with whom I ever had a sexual relationship to whom I was not physically attracted."

What did Gershwin think of his analyst? Gershwin, who was a skilled painter and draughtsman, depicted Zilboorg lying on his couch with his head resting on a cushion, almost as though he were the patient. Perhaps George wanted to suggest that analysis might have done some good for the analyst. Besides, he had already poked fun at psychoanalysis in the song "Freud and Jung and Adler", written by his brother Ira, who was clearly referring to the Warburgs undergoing analysis.

The day after George's funeral, Ira went to court to claim his brother's assets, but was contested by their mother Rose, who in the end came out on top. Peyser has pointed out that these events recall the plot of Lillian Hellman's *Little Foxes*, which appeared on Broadway in February 1939. In the play, a wife neglects her husband and denies him the medicines he needs, to obtain the wealth that would result from his death, but the inheritance is then contested by other relations. Hellman – who we have already come across in relation to the Wolf Man – was a friend of Gershwin and possibly knew the sad circumstances of George's life. But the writer also knew Zilboorg very well, having been his patient. For his part, Zilboorg claimed that he had written the successful Broadway commedy together with Hellman.

The case of George Gershwin has again uncovered the same old entanglements between patients, analysts, relations and friends involving sex and money, that are difficult to unravel. However, neurological writings have often referred to this case as a clear example of the common diagnostic error, as Peyser put it, of "an overemphasis on the patient's psychodynamics at the expense of his physical being."

Chapter 7
Why so many suicides?

Biographies of Freud constantly pose the question: why are the works of the founder of psychoanalysis so obsessed with depression and death? Particularly after the outbreak of the First World War, Freud's distress was acute. Freud found that Europe had sacrificed a culture and civilisation that went back millennia, to the "primitive impulses" of aggression and abuse of power inflicted by human beings on other human beings. Consequently, he asked people to reflect on the inevitability of warfare, and wrote in 1915 in his "Thoughts for the Times on War and Death":

> We have told ourselves, no doubt, that wars can never cease so long as nations live under such widely differing conditions, so long as the value of individual life is so variously assessed among them, and so long as the animosities which divide them represent such powerful motive forces in the mind.

He therefore argued the need to resign oneself to the inexorable nature of death: "If you want to endure life, prepare yourself for death." His concept, which recalls some of the most ancient perceptions of our world, was one in which good and evil were in everlasting conflict, and death followed life in order that life could be reborn from death. In his *Beyond the Pleasure Principle*, written in 1920, Freud distinguished between two drives: one pushing towards life and the other towards death. However, death always seems the pivot around which *becoming* evolves:

> It would be in contradiction to the conservative nature of our instincts if the goal of life were a state

153

> of things which had never yet been attained. On the
> contrary, it must be an *old* state of things, an initial
> state from which the living entity has at one time or
> other departed and to which it is striving to return ...
> If we are to take it as a truth that knows no
> exception that everything living dies for *internal*
> reasons – becomes inorganic once again – then we
> shall be compelled to say that *the aim of all life is
> death* and ... that *inanimate things existed before
> living ones.*

Precisely because of the stark recognition of the
presence of death in Freudian theory, we have to ask
ourselves whether there were any particular personal
factors and events affecting this. It has been suggested
that the sudden passing of his daughter Sophie, to
whom Freud was very close, profoundly shook and
drove him to develop fully his concept of the drive for
death. Freud rejected the personalised interpretations
which were already being aired in the twenties, but
there can be no doubt that he was profoundly affected
by a series of tragic events during the last two decades
of his life. These events concerned both public life in
general and his own private and family life.

Freud was unswerving in the thoughts on the First
World War he expressed in "Thoughts for the Times on
War and Death": "Not only is it more bloody and more
destructive than any other war of other days, because
of the enormously increased perfection of weapons of
attack and defence; it is at least as cruel, as
embittered, as implacable as any that preceded it."
Alongside this conflict, Freud had to mourn one
personal loss after another. In 1919, his pupil Viktor
Tausk committed suicide at forty. In 1920, Anton von
Freund, a close friend of Freud and a member of the
Secret Committee, died of cancer also at forty. In 1920,
his daughter Sophie died of tuberculosis aged twenty-

seven. In 1923, his dearly loved grandson and Sophie's son Heinerle died of pneumonia at four and a half years. In 1922, the daughter of his sister Rosa, Cäcilie (nicknamed Mausi), "the best of my nieces", committed suicide at the age of twenty-three because she had become pregnant while unmarried. In 1930, his niece Martha Gertrud (Tom), daughter of his sister Marie (nicknamed Mitzi), committed suicide shortly after the suicide of her husband.

Freud also experienced suffering and the progressive advance of death in his own body, from at least 1923 when it was discovered that he had a tumour. One of the most profound books on Freud, which was written by the physician Max Schur, clearly demonstrated this "dark" side to the founder father's life that continued right through from his youth to his old age: recurrent depression, psychological suffering over the death of people dear to him, physical pain from his own illness, and suicide.

The path from depression to suicide thus became a model, a style of life and death to be admired and mythologised. Freud acknowledged death on the theoretical level and placed it alongside life as the driving force behind the eternal becoming, and put forward a disenchanted concept of death (his maxim was: "If you want to able to endure life, prepare yourself for death"). But he went further and demonstrated that a human being can control his life precisely because he can freely choose his own death. It was Max Schur who administered the doses of morphine that caused Freud's death during the night of 23 September 1939, and he was the personal physician who provided the "watered-down" version of these final moments. In spite of this, the documents made public by Freud's most recent biographer, Peter Gay, demonstrate that this was not pharmacological

155

assistance for the imminent death of a semi-conscious patient, but a genuine suicide explicitly requested by someone who was still lucid. Gay interprets this deliberate choice as a stoical position – the stoics being the philosophers who controlled their own lives and deaths by an equal mix of serenity and determination. "The old stoic had kept control of his life to the end," Gay wrote of Freud's fateful decision.

Just as Freud's life and death come together in a single mythical image (he descended into the infernal depths of the soul and returned back up to reveal its secrets, ending his earthly journey in a state of complete liberty), so the history of psychoanalysis is characterised by other stories of life and death. They are striking in their tragic elements, but nevertheless do not attain the same mythical dignity. Undoubtedly melancholia and depression are also commonly found amongst psychologists. The lives of William James, Jean Piaget and Burrhus F. Skinner were marked by periods of intense depression, and these three great names are only some of many in the history of psychology. But it is equally certain that depression is even more typical of psychoanalysts. Freud, whose youthful periods of depression are known to us through his correspondence with his friend Wilhelm Fliess, compared melancholia (or depression) to mourning.

According to psychoanalysis, both mourning and depression originate from the loss of something (generally a person) with whom the subject has an emotional tie. The ego, a central structure in the psyche, triggers a series of processes to withdraw its sexual/emotional drive from the lost object, which no longer exists in reality (a dead relation or a loved person who has left). In the case of mourning, love is gradually directed towards other objects and an emotional detachment from the lost person is achieved. In the case of depression, however, the sexual/emotional drive is shifted to the ego, which is identified with the lost object. The object is not therefore lost because it has been incorporated in one's own psyche. But the relationship with oneself, which now includes the lost object, is ambivalent. There are negative charges alongside the positive emotional charges. Freud stresses that this is "the same ambivalence inherent in an amorous relationship": love and hate together. If the negative dimension is driven to its extreme and self-hate wins out, even though the self here is in the disguised form of an incorporated object, then the person concerned becomes suicidal. "The analysis of melancholia now shows that the ego can kill itself only if it can treat itself as an object – if it is able to direct against itself the hostility which relates to an object," he wrote in 1915 in *Mourning and Melancholia,* "when it can direct against itself the hostility that regards an object". Freud went further and traced a continuum joining the love of an external object to the self-hate that culminates in suicide. In both extremes, an object torments the soul: "In the two opposed situations of being most intensely in love and of suicide the ego is overwhelmed by the object, though in totally different ways."

It is difficult to say exactly what objects overwhelmed the ego of psychoanalysts. If we were to follow the reasoning of their master, it must have been the work of something that they deeply loved and at the same time hated intensely. This would have particularly been the case if, in a manner of speaking, their decision was not justified by an intolerable physical suffering, as in Freud's case. Even if we disregard the fact that many details remain obscure or unknown, partly because of immediate attempts to cover the chain of suicides with a veil of compassion, the sheer number of voluntary deaths in the psychoanalytical community is staggering (Table 1 lists the suicides and deaths in suspicious or controversial circumstances, in chronological order).

Table 1. *Suicides (or deaths considered to be suicides) committed by psychoanalysts*

1911 – Johann Jakob Honegger, pupil of Jung.
1919 – Viktor Tausk, Austrian psychoanalyst analysed by Helene Deutsch who had been analysed by Sigmund Freud.
1921 – Tatiana Rosenthal, Russian psychoanalyst
1923 – Max Kahane, Austrian psychoanalyst
1923 – Herbert Silberer, Austrian psychoanalyst
1927 – Vittorio Benussi, Italian psychologist, analysed by Otto Gross; teacher of Cesare L. Musatti
1934 – Eugénie Sokolnicka, Franco-Polish psychoanalyst, analysed by Sigmund Freud and Sándor Ferenczi
1939 – Monroe Meyer, American psychoanalyst
1940 – Sophie Morgenstern, French child psychoanalyst
1940 – Wilhelm Stekel, Austrian psychoanalyst, analysed by Sigmund Freud
1945 – Clara Happel, German psychoanalyst, analysed by Hanns Sachs
1946 – Ruth Mack Brunswick, American psychoanalyst, analysed by Sigmund Freud
1950 – Paul Federn, Austrian-American psychoanalyst, analysed by Sigmund Freud
1953 – Geza Roheim, Hungarian-American psychoanalyst, analysed by Sándor Ferenczi
1953 – Karin Stephen, English psychoanalyst
1959 – Edward Bibring, American psychoanalyst, analysed by Paul Federn (see above)
1972 – Arminda Aberastury, pioneer of Argentinian psychoanalysis
1990 – Bruno Bettelheim, American psychoanalyst

If you were to look for a common thread that links the most famous cases of depression or suicide, one candidate would be an ambivalent relationship between the victims and their analysts. From this point of view, the suicides of Tausk and Mack Brunswick immediately come to mind, as they were directly involved with Freud.

Viktor Tausk killed himself on 3 July 1919. He wrote two letters, one to his recent fiancée Hilde Loewi and one to Freud. He drank a glass of slivovitz. He then tightened a noose around his neck and shot himself in the right temple. This was a "double suicide" straight out of a textbook on legal medicine: the bullet in the head makes the body fall, ensuring death by strangulation. It is also said that Tausk castrated himself before his suicide, but we cannot be certain of this other self-destructive detail. Freud wrote an obituary in which he spoke of the originality of Tausk's work and his devotion to the psychoanalytical movement. But in a letter to Lou Andreas-Salomé, the fascinating lover of numerous famous men, starting with Nietzsche and Rilke, Freud showed another side:

> [Tausk] fought out his day of life with the father ghost. I confess I do not really miss him; I had long taken him to be useless, indeed a threat to the future.

The letter was written on 1 August 1919, a month after Tausk's suicide, and Freud displays a certain cynical lucidity in declaring that he felt no regret over the death of a supporter of psychoanalysis, particularly given the danger that he was supposed to present. Tausk's death was one of the first tragic events in the history of psychoanalysis and it triggered a process of repression that became typical of the psychoanalytical community. As is well known,

159

repression is a process described by psychoanalysis itself: it is a "defence mechanism" adopted by the psyche to keep painful events and episodes away from the conscious mind. Such events and episodes appear to have been forgotten, but remain active in the unconscious, interfere with the conscious life of the psyche and eventually explode within it. This is what happened with the Tausk case. In his public praise, Freud decreed that the whole matter was closed, using the appropriate words of admiration, but everyone knew that these were very far from the truth. In order to defend itself, psychoanalysis chose to ignore an important episode in its development, just as it would be necessary and inevitable for a child to do so during its psychological growth.

Everything is fine as long as someone or something does not cause the re-emergence of some detail that throws light on that shadowy area of the psyche. When, in 1969, Paul Roazen gathered documentary evidence on the Tausk affair and put forward some explanations of the suicide, some of which were psychoanalytical (he connected the suicide to his ambivalent relationship with Freud), repression was followed by another typical defence mechanism, resistance. Roazen was subjected to insults because what he had written about Tausk and Freud was supposed to be false. Indeed he was accused of having wormed his way into the trust of the people he interviewed, and of having used the material obtained, which was innocuous and of little significance, to fabricate fanciful and defamatory interpretations. Anna Freud's biographer, Young-Bruehl, was still referring to Roazen's book as "sloppy" and "superficial" twenty years after it was written. As soon as Anna Freud took offence with those friends and members of the psychoanalytical community who had allowed Roazen to interview them, the word went out that a new defensive wall had to be built around their "private" matters. In other words, such matters had to remain within the world of psychoanalysis.

But Roazen had done nothing more than present documents, facts and personal accounts. If he had provided groundless interpretations (not only about the Tausk affair, but also about other incidents in the history of psychoanalysis), the custodians of the psychoanalytical temple should have got on with the taks of providing the documents, facts and personal accounts that would have undermined his interpretations. Quite the opposite, they put up the usual resistance, and denied access to documents until incredibly distant dates, as though they were the most sensitive "state secrets". Roazen was absolutely right when he observed that hiding and manipulating documents attracts more attention than if the unexpurgated version had been put in the public domain.

Tausk's suicide was the result of two factors: on the one hand depression and on the other a complex tangle of emotional ties. A characteristic of Tausk's depression was its cyclical nature, which he became aware of early on, at the age of about twenty-eight, following treatment in a clinic. Insomnia afflicted him in his darkest moments, and the next day he was completely exhausted. In a letter to his wife Martha in 1907, he wrote about feeling like a "sunken human being ... physically, mentally and financially put out of action. ... Life has not shaped me, it has crushed me. I'm an ugly powerless mass, deadly tired, and I have had enough of this life."

He was unable to work, read or write. He wandered the streets without knowing where he was going, or he went straight from one cinema to another. He was

161

tormented by financial problems and questions of survival. There had been a succession of different jobs before he became a psychoanalyst, and then came the good times. It was a season of new loves, and Tausk experienced countless relationships with fascinating women. There were older and highly educated women like Lou Andreas-Salomé and younger almost illiterate women like the Serb noblewoman Kosa Latsarevich. Lea Rosen, the ballerina and actress who entered his life, was one of the reasons why he was divorced by his wife Martha. He also loved an ex-patient: the pianist Hilde Loewi, who was sixteen years younger than him. Forming stable links with a woman was a painful source of anxiety for Tausk, and fear of the imminent marriage to Hilde appears to have contributed to his final decision to commit suicide.

The fierce disagreements with Freud have been considered another reason for Tausk choosing to kill himself. There are various accounts of and explanations for this difficult teacher-pupil relationship. Lou Andreas-Salomé probably got it right when she observed that one of the major causes of discord was Tausk's ability to be ahead of Freud's ideas: the pupil was extremely adept at identifying his teacher's intuitions and new ideas, and quickly packaging them into a fully worked-out proposal. In short, Freud felt that he was being plagiarised, although he may not have been aware of it. A psychoanalytical interpretation crept into this "plagiarism".

> Only now do I perceive – Lou wrote in 1913 – the whole tragedy of Tausk's relationship with Freud: that is, I realise now that he will always tackle the same problems, the same attempts at solution, that Freud is engaged in. This is no accident, but signifies his "making himself a son" as violently as he "hates the father for it." As if by a thought-transference he

will always be busy with the same thing as Freud, never taking one step aside to make room for himself. That seemed to depend so much on the situation, but ultimately it is his own doing. ... Yet from the very beginning I realised it was this very struggle in Tausk that most deeply moved me – the struggle of the human creature. Brother-animal. You.

The teacher-pupil relationship hid a father-son conflict, and this struggle between father and son typically referred to a woman. The framework therefore corresponded to the psychoanalytical model for father-mother-son relationships, when a woman steps into the hate game between two males.

The first triangle was formed by Sigmund, Lou and Viktor. Shortly after her conversion to psychoanalysis and her move to Vienna in 1912, Lou Andreas-Salomé fell deeply in love with the "animal" Viktor or, as she described him in a letter to Freud, "a berserker with a tender heart". Lou was fifty-one and Viktor thirty-three. She was an extraordinary woman who came from Russia to cast her spell on the most famous names of Mittel-European culture. He was blond, blue-eyed, beautiful, proud and melancholic – a "beast of prey" as Sigmund had called him. Lou attended the meetings of the Psychoanalytical Society and witnessed the arguments between Viktor and Sigmund. Afterwards, she would go for dinner with the father (of psychoanalysis) and talk with him about the rebellious son. She would go to the cinema with Viktor, she would have fun with him and was happy in bed with her "brother-animal", but then she would return to the "father ghost".

The players in this psychoanalytical triangle realised they were actors in an incestuous drama, and declared themselves to be father, brother, sister or mother. You disagree with your teacher? Then this is because he symbolises the ghost of your father and evokes the unresolved conflict between father and son. You resent your pupil? Then this is because he could destroy your power, remove you from your throne and win the heart of your wife, the mother of your son.

Hence the day-to-day debate over scientific and cultural questions was overlaid with an extravagant symbolism involving imaginary fathers, mothers and children. They became trapped in a network of interpretations by which, instead of discussing real events, they argued over why people relived a repressed scene from their childhood. If you love a woman and hate a man, that is because the woman is your mother and the man is your father.

Tausk was in a state of anguish, trapped within the struggle with his teacher-father, and wanted to find a way out of this conflict. He offered his whole self to the teacher-father, and bared his soul by asking him to analyse him. However, Freud raised the stakes and sent him for analysis with Helene Deutsch, another fascinating female exponent of psychoanalysis, who had been under treatment with Freud for a few months. From one triangle to another: now it was Viktor, Helene and Sigmund. But this time the triangle had fatal consequences. Surprisingly Sigmund chose Viktor as the first patient for his patient Helene. A few months after having started her profession as an analyst, Helene had to deal with the suicide of her first patient. As Roazen remarks in his carefully documented biography, Deutsch was profoundly marked for the rest of her life by the tragic outcome of her first analysis.

Helene was not unknown to Viktor. They had been medical students together and colleagues in the same psychiatric clinic. They shared many friends and were very frequently in each other's company before starting the analysis. Helene also knew Lou, and was not very fond of her. She considered her to be a nymphomaniac who had tried to seduce her husband Felix (another analyst and also Freud's personal physician – Felix was to analyse another of Tausk's women, Lea Rosen).

In analysis Viktor talked with Helene about his relationship with Sigmund, and in turn Helene talked about the case of Viktor during her analysis with Sigmund. There came a point when it was no longer bearable and Sigmund forced Helene to accept his solution: she was to continue her analysis with him and abandon the analytical treatment she was providing Viktor. It is easy to guess who the promising psychoanalyst chose. The triangle quickly broke up. Viktor tried to replace Helene with Hilde, but could not manage to commit himself to a woman for good. A few months after analysis with Helene was broken off, Viktor killed himself. A few months after that, Sigmund suddenly broke off his analysis of Helene, which he justified by saying he had to devote all his attentions to the Wolf Man who had requested extra sessions.

"Poor Tausk," Lou wrote to Freud on hearing of the suicide, "I was fond of him. Believed I knew him; yet would never, never have thought of suicide (successful suicide – not attempts or threats I mean – strikes me almost rather as a proof of health than the contrary)." This was like saying that to demonstrate your sanity you had to overcome an unsuccessful analysis by shooting yourself in the head, and to dispel all further doubts about your mental health, you should also add a rope tied tightly around your neck.

Not everyone agreed on this original "sanity" of Tausk. In 1924, a few years after his death, the loyal Freudian Ernest Jones marked Tausk down as a "a paraphrenic who could come to no other end." Tausk a paraphrenic or schizophrenic? How do we reconcile the presence of this disorder with the fact that Tausk's greatest contribution was precisely his attempt to provide a psychoanalytical explanation of schizophrenia?

Here we encounter a significant problem: the relationship between one's own psychological illness and the object of one's research. We study and explain the things that affect us. This observation is far from original, and is often voiced in faculties of psychology where emaciated girls submit yet more theses on anorexia and less undernourished ones submit theses on obesity. It is no surprise then that the most important psychoanalytical theorisation of depression was provided by Melanie Klein, who notoriously suffered from acute attacks of depression. Melanie's biographer, Phyllis Grosskurth, has quite rightly written that *"The Psychogenesis of Manic-Depressive States* is an exploration of Klein's psyche. ... In manic-depressive illness there is a dread that one contains dying or dead objects." Melanie met many real or imaginary dying objects during her life: at the age of four her sister Sidonie died, at eighteen her father, and at twenty her brother Emanuel, who suffered from manic-depressive psychosis and to whom Melanie was morbidly attached. Grosskurth wrote: "Brother and sister, they were twin souls, sharing the same sort of moods and reactions. He was her surrogate father, close companion, phantom lover – and no one in her life was ever able to replace him." We can add Karl Abraham to this chain of death. He had started analysis with her a few months earlier ("a great pain for me and a very painful situation to come through"). Lastly, we could add her son Hans, who died at twenty-seven in an accident (but his sister Melitta and other psychoanalysts believed it was suicide).

The periods of depression became more acute during such events, but also occurred during pregnancy. Melanie suffered from despair at these times and cried uncontrollably, and in 1909 she underwent two months of treatment for depression in a Swiss clinic. We can only conclude that Klein's famous studies on depression, anxiety and bereavement were nothing more than the psychoanalyst revisiting her inner struggles and her ways of overcoming them. According to Klein's perception, depression should be seen as a necessary moment in psychological development, and the pain associated with it is required to attain psychological maturity. Her friend and assistant Joan Riviere pointed out to Melanie in a letter in 1940 that people tend "to feel, as M. [Melitta, her daughter] obviously does, that your views represent a wish to force depression on everybody." Indeed Klein's thought does not so much reflect recognition of the inevitable presence of pain and death in the life of every human being as how that inevitability can be transformed into a conceptual system. (Her mother Libussa had already made the former proposition clear to her many years before: "One has to put up with all those little mosquito bites and vexations of life without getting upset. We should look upon them as the darkness without which there can be no light"). Hence weeping in the face of death is no longer an emotion, but only a perturbation in the face of a natural phenomenon, similar to that which may be experienced when observing rapids or a volcano erupting. It is no surprise then that those deaths became "objects" that parade across the psyche's inner stage as though they are actors in a play in which we are not involved.

There was talk of suicide in the case of another of Sigmund Freud's loyal followers: Ruth Mack. Ruth's second marriage was to Mark Brunswick, and she became known as Mack Brunswick. Mark was in analysis with Sigmund Freud, as was his brother David. Ruth started analysis with Freud in 1922. The relationships were extremely complex in this case as well: Sigmund Freud analysed two brothers (Mark and David) and one of their wives (Ruth), while she analysed Freud's doctor, Max Schur, and his wife Helen. Ruth Mack Brunswick became famous, as has been previously stated, for being the Wolf Man's second analyst. She was also Muriel Gardiner's analyst, and both friend and benefactor of this famous patient.

In other words, it was one big family. Freud had had Sergey Konstantinovich Pankeyev (the Wolf Man) as his patient, and he also knew his wife Teresa, but he also had Ruth, Sergey's analyst, as his own patient. Freud also knew the husband Mark well, because he too was one of his patients. As has been stated on many occasions, the analysts knew husbands and wives, whether or not they were patients. The Viennese journalist Karin Obholzer once asked Sergey Konstantinovich about his habit of going with prostitutes, to which Ruth had referred. To the first question about whether his wife knew, Sergey Konstantinovich commented: "Of course not. Other men do the same". To the second question about whether Ruth personally acquainted with his wife, the Wolf Man replied:

> Yes, I can't remember why, but she once told me that I had to come with Teresa. Then she told [me]: "She's not at all beautiful." She had something

against my wife. I think she was jealous because
Freud had praised her. You know what women are
like, even when they are psychoanalysts.

Insufficient attention has been paid to the fact that
Ruth was also the analyst of Robert Fliess, the son of
Wilhelm, Freud's great friend. Before his analysis with
Ruth, Robert had been analysed by Karl Abraham in
Berlin. Then he moved to the United States where he
felt the need for deeper analysis. Who knows whether
the memory of sexual abuse by his father came to the
surface during this second treatment. Reality or
fantasy? For Jeffrey Masson, who has studied the
period leading up to the birth of psychoanalysis in
depth, it is fairly likely that it was a real event. When
Freud abandoned his "seduction theory" (according to
which neurosis in adulthood originates in actual
sexual abuse suffered during childhood at the hands of
adults, sometimes parents or close relations), he is
supposed to have commented upon his research into
sexual seduction with Wilhelm Fliess, the least
suitable person. "Freud was like a dogged detective",
Masson wrote, "on the track of a great crime,
communicating his hunches and approximations and
at last his final discovery to his best friend, who may
have been in fact the criminal."

Ruth came to know of another case of abuse: the
Wolf Man is also supposed to have been sodomised by
a relation when he was little. However, she did not
inform Freud of this, and according to Masson, he may
have known already, but pretended not to, in order to
avoid having to alter his interpretation of Sergey
Konstantinovich Pankeyev's neurosis as the result of
witnessing a scene involving his parents.

Did Ruth tell Freud about little Robert being abused
in his family? One thing we can be certain of is that
information and gossip, as we might call it, must have

circulated very easily, given the tangle of kinship and analysis. For example, Ruth was in analysis with Herman Nunberg after her analysis with Sigmund Freud. Who was this Herman? He was Margarethe Rie's husband, and Margarethe's mother was Melanie, who was the sister of Ida who married Wilhelm Fliess, the marriage that produced Robert. Herman Nunberg was analysed by Paul Federn, who possibly received some form of analysis from Freud. Nunberg, in turn, analysed the son of Paul Federn, Ernst, who was also to become a psychoanalyst, and Ruth Mack Brunswick, who in turn had been analysed by Freud and was to analyse Robert Fliess. Robert Fliess was a cousin of Nunberg, because he married Robert's cousin Margarethe Rie, and Margarethe had been analysed by Freud as had her sister, Marianne, the wife of Ernst Kris, who in turn was analysed by Helene Deutsch, who was analysed by Sigmund Freud, whose suicidal niece Cäcilie had been analysed by Paul Federn (Fig. 6).

We can go on. Ruth, "an orthodox psycho-analyst" (we have Sergey Konstantinovich Pankeyev's word for it) had a passion for barbiturates, and she gradually moved on to morphine. She was sometimes so overcome by drugs that she would fall asleep on the bathroom floor. Her death, which came in 1946, was attributed to a heart attack. It is alleged however that, stupefied by narcotics as was her habit, she slipped in the bathroom and banged her head. P. Roazen reports that "Mark said she died from a fall that fractured her skull, but that it was not a suicide."

The most spectacular suicide – and here unfortunately the adjective is required – was that of Herbert Silberer, one of the first members of the Viennese Psychoanalytical Society. His depression became so bad after his break with Freud that, in

1923 at the age of forty-one, he hung himself from the bars of a window. Before this insane gesture, however, he had arranged an electric torch so the light fell directly on his face. Thus, when his wife returned, she immediately saw his expression in death. One of the most sympathetic obituaries for Silberer was written by Wilhelm Stekel, who was also one of the first members of the Freudian circle, and soon to break with Freud. He also committed suicide, albeit in a less theatrical manner. In 1940, he injected himself with a large dose of insulin.

For decades very little was known about these tragic deaths outside the psychoanalytical community, which tried to keep the skeletons firmly locked in the cupboard. In this case, the metaphor almost reflects the reality. When, on 13 March 1990, Bruno Bettelheim killed himself by pulling a plastic bag over his head after having taken several alcoholic drinks and barbiturates, he probably dealt the final blow to the image of psychoanalysis as a model of psycho-logical growth. Bettelheim's notoriety outside the world of specialists and the climate of increasing hostility towards psychoanalysis meant that his case was splashed across every newspaper. There was a wave of truths and lies for and against him, as he was considered something of a "guru", and this soon involved the rest of the psychoanalytical movement. Nina Sutton's excellent biography of him has very effectively portrayed a complex figure. Bettelheim, who was deported to Dachau and Buchenwald, is supposed to have treated the little boarders at his school for children with mental disorders in the manner of a Nazi regime. He studied fairy tales, and transformed the "enchanted world" into an actual world of fear and intimidation meted out to his patients on a daily basis. He stalked the famous Orthogenic School of Chicago

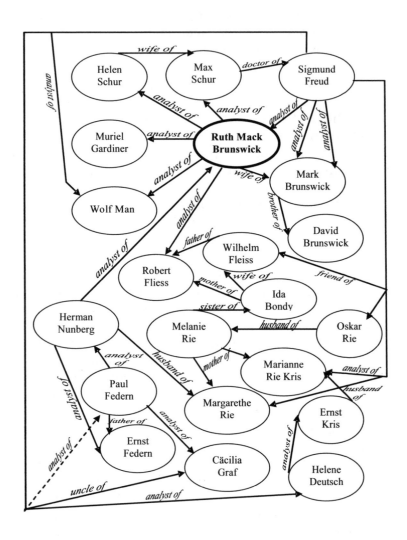

Fig. 6. The constellation of Ruth Mack Brunswick

like a "big bad wolf". So much for fairy tales! In the letters and articles that appeared after his death, many ex-patients, now adults, felt as though they had been freed from a terrible weight. They had finally understood: "A plastic bag, you've got to be kidding! ... I have to talk to the others. He was crazy!" was a comment that we find in Sutton's biography. "When I think of all he said to me! And all that time HE was the crazy one...Do you hear? He was mad, NOT ME." Not only was he mad, they said, he was also violent: he would beat children. Because of his alleged brutality, he was called "Beno Brutalheim" in a *Newsweek* headline in September 1990, which added a meaningful comment: "He had seen a dictator who destroyed people, and he became a dictator who wanted to rescue people." The title of one of his most famous books, *Love is Not Enough*, now took on another meaning that implied a need for violent and authoritarian therapies and educational systems.

If Bettelheim had not been a psychoanalyst, his suicide would not have caused such a stir. It would have been said that he was simply a depressed old man, who was desolate after the death of his wife. He was ill and deserted within an old people's home, albeit a very luxurious one. But he was a psychoanalyst, a scientist who had authoritatively explained the strategies that the mind can and must adopt to confront fear, anxiety and violence. He had really believed in this. For some people, this showed that the psychological structure developed through psycho-analytical training was not therefore very solid, and it was not a real instrument for survival.

Finally there is a suicide with which psychoanalysis has a paradoxical relationship, or at least a symbolic one, in the sense that suicide can have the purpose of avoiding a psychotherapeutic relationship. At secondary school and during his early years at university, Sigmund Freud developed a close friendship with Eduard Silberstein. They compared themselves to the two dogs in a novella by Cervantes who discussed the miseries of life (Sigmund took the name of the dog called Scipio and Eduard that of Braganza). In their letters they talked about their intellectual interests and their romantic hopes. Their lives then took different paths but they stayed in contact (Silberstein became a banker with strong social and political commitments). Thus, when Eduard's first wife, Paula (known as Pauline) Theiler started to show signs of mental imbalance, her husband advised her to visit his old friend Sigmund.

The first visit was supposed to take place in 1891, during the period in which Freud was treating cases of hysteria with the technique of hypnosis and had not yet developed the principles and methods of psychoanalysis. Pauline went to the building where Freud lived and received his patients. She climbed the stairs, and stopped at the third floor, but was unable to knock on the door of her husband's medical friend. She threw herself out of the window and died on impact. For her psychoanalysis would not have brought any relief.

Epilogue

An enormous goldfish comes crashing down on a town square. A little girl with blond bobbed hair is crushed and raises her hands to the sky in desperation. The fish itself looks stunned and its large eyes are opened wide. The surrounding buildings start to crack, and at any moment they will collapse. On top of a roof, a cat with its back arched watches with curiosity. It will perhaps be the only survivor of this catastrophe. In the background, a silvery moon tells us that it is night.

These images appear in an illustration for a children's book called *Die Fischereise* (*The Fish's Journey*), which was published in Berlin in 1923. The colours are vivid. The fish is tomato red, the little girl's dress is blue and her hat is brown, while the cat is yellow and the buildings that are about to crumble are purple, ochre and green. The artist was Martha Gertrud, Sigmund Freud's niece, better known as Tom Seidmann-Freud. She preferred to use a man's name and wear men's clothes because she felt she was more of a man than a woman, in spite of being married to the journalist Jankew Seidmann who published her books. Tom illustrated many books for children including one about her dreams. Her magnificent books were banned and destroyed by the Nazis, because she was Jewish, and now they are very rare and worth more on the second-hand book market than first editions of her uncle Sigmund's works. Jankew killed himself on 19 October 1929, and Tom, who was suffering from deep depression, committed suicide on 7 February 1930, when she was only thirty-seven. An awkward member of the Freud family, Tom hardly gets a mention in the vast reams of Freudian literature.

When I saw the picture of the goldfish for the first time, it gave me the same sense of unease I felt when reading books and articles on the lives of psychoanalysts. The deeper I went into the complex and tragic stories of their lives, the more I had this feeling of impending catastrophe. When psychoanalysis shattered the stained-glass windows of the Western psyche's fortified citadel, it revealed the rottenness and anguish that dwelt within. That psyche was like a huge fish in a small bowl, and once psychoanalysts had provoked it, it thrashed around, removed the water and then lay dying while its fins vainly flapped on the bottom. By so doing, however, psychoanalysts appear to have created the conditions for their own demise.

When psychoanalysis came to be considered a "world view", a philosophical concept or even for some a new mythology, Freud reacted very strongly claiming that, quite the contrary, he had established a rigorous science for the study of the restricted field of psychological processes, and he had no intention of encroaching upon the wider spheres of philosophy or religion. Philosophers and psychologists willing to discuss this restricted field (psychoanalysis as a science) posed the question of whether theoretical and practical psychoanalysis had in fact adhered to scientific rules. From this point of view, it is understandable that psychoanalysis had to be evaluated just like any other theoretical or therapeutic formulation by posing the question of whether its theoretical principles have any foundation. Do they have any connection to concepts and principles found in other approaches, for example in psychology, psychiatry, biology or neuroscience? Is psychoanalytical therapy effective? Has the appropriate research been carried out, as in other scientific fields, to verify the efficacy of the treatment and the absence of relapses? The replies have been varied.

This debate, although both interesting and necessary, failed to consider a fundamental aspect of psychoanalysis, or at the very most only touched on it. That aspect was the personal, biographical, historical and cultural dimension of its exponents. It is often argued that this or that theory or discovery loses none of its historical or scientific value if some scandalous or aberrant fact is discovered when people start scouring through the private vices and family wrangles of the famous scientist responsible for the theory or discovery. In the case of psychoanalysis, however, no such argument can be applied. A psychoanalyst's life becomes directly involved in the theory and practice. It either substantiates them or it destroys them. Bettelheim declared with apparent confidence:

> The difference between the patient and the therapist is that the therapist can at will walk back and forth across the bridge. He knows at any one moment how far he can safely venture into the chaotic world across the river that separates sanity from insanity, as he knows when to beat a quick retreat from this alien territory back into the sane world

The therapist can wander back and forth across the bridge between reason and folly, checking up on those who find themselves on one or other side and at the same time checking up on himself. You get the impression that some of the great figures in the history of psychoanalysis lost their own by endlessly rushing one way and then the other, over that bridge built across the torments of hell. Yet some hard-boiled and insensitive critic might suggest that the bridge

177

(representing psychoanalytical theory and therapy) was not strong enough and inevitably had to collapse, taking both analyst and patient with it. In short, the theory and practice of psychoanalysis have been built on shaky foundations and the lives of psychoanalysts have been entwined with the lives of their patients. As Giovanni Jervis has written, the history of psychoanalysis has been "the history of a series of makeshift generalisations that emerged from a complex tangle of experiences and personal and interpersonal problems concerning psychoanalysts and their patients".

We can distinguish between two critical approaches to relationships between the lives and personalities of psychoanalysts and the theoretical and therapeutic model adopted by psychoanalysis. According to the first approach (which we shall call "biographical"), the limitations of psychoanalysis result from on weaknesses in the analyst who is unable to control his own psyche properly, while its fundamental principles are still valid. Once you have removed the classical and pioneering phase of psychoanalysis in which "errors" at a personal level were inevitable, you can then demonstrate its solid conceptual and practical structure. The second approach (which we shall call "theoretical and scientific") argues that it is precisely the theoretical and therapeutic fragility of psychoanalysis that inevitably led to unfavourable effects on the psychological life of its followers.

The philosopher Frank Cioffi has recently challenged the reliability of the discoveries that Freud and other psychoanalysts are supposed to have achieved in analytical sessions and faithfully reported in their publications (you are reminded of the matter of "invented cases"). The biographical dimension is therefore of fundamental importance. Cioffi argues that psychoanalysis is a science based on the evidence of witnesses and on the trust that can be placed on them. The key witness is the psychoanalyst. You either take him at his word when he tells you what has been discovered under analysis or you don't, and it all revolves around his perception as a witness. There is no public demonstration of its assertions, as required by modern science. As the poet Paul Celan has said, "in as much as no one bears witness to the witness, who will bear witness to the psychoanalyst?

Within the "theoretical and scientific" approach, there are those like Adolf Grünbaum, another philosopher of science, who argue that the debate should be restricted to the theoretical dimension and the empirical verification of psychoanalysis, leaving aside the biographic vicissitudes of its followers. You could argue a simpler theory that reconciles these two critical approaches, the biographical and the theoretical and scientific. Firstly, there is no psychoanalysis that can be separated from the psychological life of its founders and exponents. Secondly, psychoanalysis has shown itself to be a weak theory precisely because those who created it were not strong enough to sustain the complexity of their own psychological lives that unravelled and unveiled themselves while the theory itself was being applied.

Who would try to treat a tumour by cutting open their own body with their own hands, in the attempt to separate the healthy tissues from the diseased ones, while the hands become saturated with malignant cells? No one would expect to survive such an operation. Then again, the hands may have been diseased even before attempting to carry out surgery on one's own or someone else's psyche. Any disinfectant would only increase the pain and every further operation would only deepen the surgeon's wound. This is no false analogy. It was suggested by Freud who liked to compare the surgeon and the analyst, and wrote in *Recommendations to Physicians Practising Psycho-Analysis* (1912):

> I cannot advise my colleagues too urgently to model themselves during psychoanalytical treatment on the surgeon, who puts aside all his feelings, even his human sympathy, and concentrates his mental forces on the single aim of performing the operation as skilfully as possible.

As we have seen, there was no lack of "feelings" and "human sympathy" in the relationship between analyst and patient throughout the history of psychoanalysis. Thus the fears that Freud expressed in *Analysis Terminable and Interminable* (1937) were to come true: x-rays are used for discovering illness and treating the patient, but at the same time the radiation makes the doctor ill. For this reason, Freud's essay suggested the need for the analyst to undergo regular decontamination. Like the cat in Tom's illustration, Freud continued to look down from above. He will be the last to fall and, in a typically catlike manner, he will land on his feet. Inscrutable to the end, he wanders amongst the rubble, guided by the light of the full moon.

Sources and bibliographical notes

Chapter One (pp. 1-36)

Quotations in the text were taken from:
D. Bertelsen, *Alltag bei Familie Freud: Die Erinnerungen der Paula Fichtl* (Hamburg: Hoffmann und Camp Verlag, 1987);
S. Farber and M. Green, *Hollywood on the Couch: A Candid Look at the Overheated Love Affair between Psychiatrists and Moviemakers* (New York: William Morrow and Company, Inc., 1993);
R.S. Greenson, *Technique and Practice in Psychoanalysis* (London: Hogarth Press, 1967);
L. Pepitone, W. Stadiem and M. C. Hakim, *Marilyn Confidential* (New York: Simon & Schuster, 1979);
D. Spoto, *Marilyn Monroe: the Biography* (London: Arrow, 1994);
D.H. Wolfe, *The Assassination of Marilyn Monroe* (London: Warner, 1999);
E. Young-Bruehl, *Anna Freud: A Biography* (London: W. W. Norton, 1988).

The following works have been used for the life of Marilyn Monroe: M. Monroe, *My Story* (New York: Stein and Day, 1974); E. Murray (co-authored by R. Shade), *Marilyn: The Last Months* (New York: Pyramid Books, 1975); L. Pepitone, W. Stadiem and M.C. Hakim, *Marilyn Confidential* (New York: Simon & Schuster, 1979); D. Spoto, *Marilyn Monroe: the Biography* (London: Arrow, 1994); and above all the biography written by D.H. Wolfe, which concentrates on reconstructing events during the last few days of Marilyn Monroe's life, *The Assassination of Marilyn Monroe* (London: Warner, 1999). V. Adam, *The Marilyn Encyclopaedia* (New York: Overlook Press, 1999) is an essential source of information. The portrait of Marilyn provided by M. V. Montalbán in *El hermano pequeño* (1994) is pleasant and psychologically interesting. While the original Italian version of this book was being printed in 2000, *Blonde. A novel* by J. C. Oates (New York: Echo Press, 2000) was published, and contains an insightful analysis of Marilyn's psyche. Other more recent works include: M. Smith, *Marilyn's Last Words: Her Secret Tapes and Mysterious Death* (New York: Carroll and Graf, 2004); M. Morgan, *Marilyn Monroe: Private and Undisclosed* (New York: Carroll and Graf, 2007); M. Schneider, *Marilyn: Dernières séances* (Paris: Bernard Grasset, 2008). For a psychoanalytical interpretation of Marilyn's inner life and behaviour, see A. Jacke, *Marilyn Monroe und die Psychoanalyse* (Giessen: Psychosozial-Verlag, 2005).

For the spread of psychoanalysis amongst film-industry circles in Hollywood, the fundamental work is S. Farber and M. Green, *Hollywood on the Couch: A Candid Look at the Overheated Love Affair between Psychiatrists and Moviemakers* (New York: William Morrow and Company, Inc., 1993). See also H.R. Greenberg, *Screen Memories. Hollywood Cinema on the Psychoanalytic Couch* (New York: Columbia University Press, 1993).

For Marilyn Monroe's psychoanalysts, particularly R.S. Greenson, extensive material can be found in the biographies referred to above and in Farber and Green, *Hollywood on the Couch.*

R.S. Greenson's works include *Explorations in Psychoanalysis* (New York: Intl. Universities Press, 1978) and *Technique and Practice in Psychoanalysis* (London: Hogarth Press, 1967). His essay on *Special Problems in Psychotherapy with the Rich and Famous*, which was written in 1978, has been partially reprinted in Spoto, *Marilyn Monroe: the Biography.* D. Kirsner has produced two highly relevant papers on Greenson and his analysis of Marilyn: "Politics Masquerading as Science: Ralph Greenson, Anna Freud and the Klein wars", *The Psychoanalytical Review* 93 (2005), pp. 907-27; "Do As I

Say, Not As I Do: Ralph Greenson, Anna Freud and Super-rich Patients", *Psychoanalytical Psychology*, 24 (2007), pp. 475-86.

For the relationship between Marilyn Monroe and Anna Freud, see D. Berthelsen, *Alltag bei Familie Freud. Die Erinnerungen der Paula Fichtl* (Hamburg: Hoffmann und Campe Verlag, 1987), a book based on the memoirs of the housekeeper Paula Fichtl, and E. Young-Bruehl, *Anna Freud: a Biography* (London: W.W. Norton, 1988).

On the groups of psychoanalysts linked to Fenichel and the question of the relationship with Marxism and the Communist party, see not only Wolfe's recent biography of Marilyn, but also the fundamental work by R. Jacoby, *The Repression of Psychoanalysis: Otto Fenichel and the Political Freudians* (Chicago: University of Chicago Press, 1983).

Chapter Two (pp. 37-58)

Quotations in the text are from:

H. Abraham, "Karl Abraham: An Unfinished Biography", *International Review of Psychoanalysis*, 1 (1974), pp. 17-72;

A. Freud, *Beating Fantasies and Daydreams* (1922), in *Writings*, Vol. 1 (New York: International Universities Press, 1974);

S. Freud, *The Selected Letters* (New York: Basic Books, 1960);

P. Grosskurth, *Melanie Klein: Her World and Her Work* (New York: Hodder & Stoughton, 1986);

C. G. Jung, *Psychic Conflicts in a Child* (1910), in *Collected Works*, Vol. 17, *The Development of Personality* (London: Routledge & Kegan Paul, 1954);

M. Klein. *The Writings of Melanie Klein* (London: Hogarth Press and the Institute of Psychoanalysis, 1975);

E. Young-Bruehl, *Anna Freud: A Biography* (London: W. W. Norton, 1988).

On Anna Freud: P. Roazen, *Brother Animal: the Story of Freud and Tausk* (New York: New York Universities Press, 1969); P. Roazen, *Freud and his Followers* (New York: Knopf, 1975); D. Berthelsen, *Alltag bei Familie Freud. Die Erinnerungen der Paula Fichtl* (Hamburg: Hoffmann und Campe Verlag, 1987); E. Young-Bruehl, *Anna Freud: a Biography* (London: W. W. Norton, 1988); P. Roazen, *Meeting Freud's Family* (Massachusetts: University of Massachusetts, 1993). Interesting personal memories can be found in E. Binswanger, *Reminiscences of a Friendship* (New York: Grune & Stratton, 1956); E. Weiss, *Sigmund Freud as a Consultant: Recollections of a Pioneer in Psychoanalysis* (New York: International Medical Book Corp. 1970). See also A. Freud, *Beating Fantasies and Daydreams* (1922), in *Writings*, Vol. 1, (New York: International Universities Press, 1974). Sigmund Freud's letter on homosexuality is in *The Selected Letters* (New York: Basic Books, 1960).

On Dorothy Burlingham: apart from the previously mentioned works of Berthelsen, Young-Bruehl and Roazen, see M. Burlingham, *The Last Tiffany: A Biography of Dorothy Tiffany Burlingham* (New York: Atheneum, 1989).

On Melanie Klein: P. Grosskurth, *Melanie Klein: Her World and Her Work* (New York: Hodder & Stoughton, 1986). The analyses of her children are described in M. Kein's early works, collected in *The Writings of Melanie Klein* (London: Hogarth Press and the Institute of Psychoanalysis, 1975; reprinted in *Love, Guilt and Reparation and Other Works 1921-1945*, New York: Dell Publ., 1977).

On Hilda Doolittle: H. Doolittle, *Tribute to Freud* (Manchester: Carcanet, 1985); S. Stanford Friedman,

Psyche Reborn. The Emergence Of H.D. (Bloomington: Indiana University Press, 1981).

On Karl Abraham: H. Abraham, "Karl Abraham: An Unfinished Biography", *International Review of Psychoanalysis*, 1 (1974), pp. 17-72. Hilda is spoken about in K. Abraham, "Little Hilda: Daydreams and symptoms in a seven-year-old girl", *International Review of Psychoanalysis*, 1 (1974), pp. 5-14. There is also a reference to Hilda in *Selected Papers* (New York: Basic Books, 1957).

For Carl Gustav Jung, see the *Sources* for Chapter Three. The analysis of Jung's daughters is described in C.G. Jung, *Psychic Conflicts in a Child* (1910) in *Collected Works*, Vol. 17, *The Development of Personality* (London: Routledge & Kegan Paul 1954).

Chapter Three (pp. 59-98)

Quotations in the text are from:

Carotenuto, *A Secret Symmetry: Sabina Spielrein between Jung and Freud* (New York: Pantheon Books, 1982);

The Correspondence of Sigmund Freud and Sándor Ferenczi 1908-1914, Vol. 1 (Cambridge: The Belknap Press of Harvard University Press, 1994);

C. Douglas, *Translate the Darkness: The Life of Christiana Morgan: The Veiled Woman in Jung's Circle* (New York: Simon & Schuster, 1993);

The Freud/Jung Letters, ed. W. McGuire (London: Penguin, 1991);

S. Freud, "Fragment of an Analysis of a Case of Hysteria" (1905) in *The standard edition of the Complete Psychological Works of Sigmund Freud*, Vol. 7 (London: Hogarth Press, 1957);

S. Freud, "Observations on Transference-Love" (1915), in *The standard edition of the Complete Psychological Works of Sigmund Freud*, Vol. 12 (London: Hogarth Press, 1957);

E. Fromm, *The Art of Loving* (London: Thorsons, 1995).

E. Jones, *Free Associations: Memoirs of a Psychoanalyst* (New York: Basic Books, 1959);

C. G. Jung, *The Freudian Theory of Hysteria* (1907), in *The Collected Works of C. G. Jung. Vol. 4. Freud and Psychoanalysis* (London: Routledge & Kegan Paul, 1961, pp. 10-24);

R. Michels, *Psicoanalisi dell'amore,* in D. N. Stern and M. Ammaniti (a cura di), *Psicoanalisi dell'amore*, Laterza, Roma-Bari, 1993;

A. Nin, *Incest* (London: Peter Owen, 1993);

R. Noll, *The Jung Cult: Origins of a Charismatic Movement* (New York: Free Press, 1979);

P. Roazen, *Helen Deutsch: A Psychoanalyst's Life* (New York: Anchor Press, 1985);

F. G. Robinson, *Love's Story Told: A Life of Henry A. Murray* (Cambridge: Harvard University Press, 1992).

For the relationship between Sigmund Freud and his sister-in-law Minna, see J.M. Billinsky, "Jung and Freud (The End of a Romance)", *Andover Newton Quarterly*, vol. 10(2), (1969), pp. 39-43; P. Roazen, *Freud and His Followers* (New York: Knopf, 1975); P. J. Swales, "Freud, Minna Bernays, and the Conquest of Rome", *New American Review*, Vol. 1 (1982), pp. 1-23; K. R. Eissler, *Three Instances of Injustice* (New York: International Universities Press, 1970).

For Gross, see Marianne Weber, *Max Weber. A Biography* (New Brunswick: Transaction Publishers, 1988); E. Hurwitz, *Otto Gross: "Paradies"-Sucher zwischen Freud und Jung* (Zurich-Frankfurt: Suhrkamp Verlag, 1979); M. Green, *The Von Richtofen Sisters. The Triumphant and the Tragic Modes of Love* (New York: Basic Books, 1974); J. Le Rider, *Otto Gross: Revolution sur le divan* (Paris: Solin, 1988); R. Noll, *The Jung Cult: Origins of a Charismatic Movement* (New York: Free Press, 1997). Apart from the bibliography provided by Noll, see also T. Anz, "Jemand mußte Otto G. veleumdet haben ... Kafka, Weifel, Otto Gross und eine «psychiatrische Geschichte»", *Akzente*, vol. 31(2), (1984), pp. 184-191. M. Green, *Otto Gross. Freudian Psychoanalyst, 1877-1920* (Lewinston, N.Y.: Queenston, 1999).

On Jung: B. Hannah, *Jung: His Life and Works. A Biographical Memory* (New York: G. P. Putnam's Sons, 1976); R. Noll, *The Jung Cult. Origins of a Charismatic Movement* (New York: Free Press, 1979); N. Neri, *Oltre l'ombra. Donne intorno a Jung* (Rome: Borla, 1995); F. McLynn, *Carl Gustav Jung. A Biography* (London: Bantam Press, 1997); D. Blair, *Jung. A Biography* (New York: Little, Brown, 2003).

On Spielrein: *The Freud/Jung Letters*, ed. W. McGuire (London: Penguin, 1991); C.G. Jung, *The Freudian Theory of Hysteria* (1907) in *The Collected Works of C. G. Jung*, Vol. 4, *Freud and Psychoanalysis* (London: Routledge & Kegan Paul, 1961), pp. 10-24; A. Carotenuto, *A Secret Symmetry. Sabina Spielrein between Jung and Freud* (New York: Pantheon Books, 1982), which also contains an essay by B. Bettelheim, letters from Spielrein to Jung and Freud, letters from Freud to Spielrein and Spielrein's *Diary*; A. Etkind, *Eros of the Impossible: The History of Psychoanalysis in Russia* (New York: Westview Press, 1997); N. Kerr, *A Most Dangerous Method: The Story of Jung, Freud and Sabina Spielrein* (New York: Knopf, 1993); Z. Lothane, "In defense of Sabina Spielrein", in P. Mahony, C. Bonomi, J. Stensson (eds.), *Behind the Scenes. Freud in Correspondence* (Oslo: Scandinavian University Press, 1997), pp. 81-109; C. Covington and B. Wharton (eds.), *Sabina Spielrein. Forgotten Pioneer of Psychoanalysis* (New York: Routledge, 2003).

On Murray and Morgan: F.G. Robinson, *Love's Story Told. A Life of Henry A. Murray* (Cambridge: Harvard University Press, 1992); C. Douglas, *Translate the Darkness. The Life of Christiana Morgan. The Veiled Woman in Jung's Circle* (New York: Simon & Schuster,

1993). Morgan's visions are described and commented upon in C.G. Jung, *Vision Seminars* (Princeton: Princeton University Press, 1997).

On Ferenczi: *The Correspondence of Sigmund Freud and Sándor Ferenczi 1908-1914*, Vol. I (Cambridge: Harvard University Press, 1994); L. Aron and A. Harris (eds.), *The Legacy of Sándor Ferenczi* (Hillsdale, NJ: Analytic Press, 1993); G. Antonelli, *Il mare di Ferenczi. La storia, il pensiero, la tecnica di un maestro della psicoanalisi* (Rome: Di Renzo Editore, 1997); C. Bonomi, "Jones's allegation of Ferenczi's mental deterioration", *International Journal of Psychoanalysis*, Vol. 80 (1999), pp. 507-42. P.L. Rudnyntsky, A. Bókay and P. Giampieri-Deutsch (eds.), *Ferencszi's Turn in Psychoanalysis* (New York: New York University Press, 2000); P.L. Rudnytsky, *Reading Psychoanalysis: Freud, Rank, Ferenczi and Groddeck* (Ithaca & London: Cornell University Press, 2002).

On Balint: A. Haynal, *The Technique at Issue: Controversies in Psychoanalysis from Freud and Ferenczi to Michael Balint* (London: Karnak, 1988).

On Radó: P. Roazen, *Helene Deutsch. A Psychoanalyst's Life* (New York: Anchor Press, 1985); P. Roazen and B. Swerdloff, *Heresy: Sándor Radó and the Psychoanalytical Movement* (New Jersey: Jason Aronson, 1995).

On Eitingon: J.J. Dziak, *Chekisty: A History of the KGB* (Lexington: Lexington Books, 1987); A. Etkind, *Eros of the Impossible: The History of Psychoanalysis in Russia* (New York: Westview Press, 1997).

On Allendy, Rank and Anaïs Nin: J. Taft, *Otto Rank* (New York: The Julian Press, 1958); A. Nin, *Incest* (London: Peter Owen, 1993); P.L. Rudnytsky, *Reading Psychoanalysis: Freud, Rank, Ferenczi, Groddeck* (Ithaca & London: Cornell University Press, 2002).

On Jones: E. Jones, *Free Associations. Memoirs of a Psychoanalyst* (New York: Basic Books, 1959). B.

Maddox, *Freud's Wizard: Ernest Jones and the Transformation of Psychoanalysis* (Cambridge, MA: Da Capo Press, 2007).

For romantic attachments between analysts and patients through the interpretative framework of the concepts of transference and counter-transference, the most systematic study is G. O. Gabbard and E.P. Lester, *Boundaries and Boundary Violations in Psychoanalysis* (New York: Basic Books, 1996). See also the essays by A. Haynal, A.M. Cooper, R. Michels, G. Di Chiara and M. Mancia, in D.N. Stern and M. Ammaniti (eds.), *Psicoanalisi dell'amore* (Roma-Bari: Laterza, 1993). Of course Freud's writings are still fundamental, and of particular note is *Observations on Transference-Love* (1915), in S. Freud, *The standard edition of the Complete Psychological Works of Sigmund Freud* (London: Hogarth Press, 1957), Vol. 12, pp. 156-173.

The biographical entries contained in E. Roudinesco and M. Plon, *Dictionnaire de la psychanalyse* (Paris: Fayard, 1997) are very useful, as well as those in A. de Mijolla (ed.), *International Dictionary of Psychoanalysis*, 3 vols. (Detroit: Thomson Gale, 2005). Two fundamental works are F. Alexander, S. Eisenstein and M. Grotjahn (eds.), *Psychoanalytic Pioneers* (New York: Basic Books, 1966) and P. Roazen, *Freud and his Followers* (New York: Knopf, 1975).

On relations between psychoanalysts and patients in Hollywood, see S. Farber and M. Green, *Hollywood on the Couch: A Candid Look at the Overheated Love Affair between Psychiatrists and Moviemakers* (New York: Willam Morrow and Co., 1993).

On the cinematographic representation of these relationships, see G.O. Gabbard and K. Gabbard, *Psychiatry and the Cinema* (Washington Psychiatric Press: American Psychiatric Press, 1999).

On Fromm, see P. Roazen, "Il coraggio di Erich Fromm", *Psicoterapia e Scienze Umane*, 3 (1998), pp.

15-39. Cf. E. Fromm, *The Art of Loving* (London: Thorsons, 1995).

Freud on the reasons why the "complications" cannot be separated from psychoanalytical method, see Freud, *Analysis of a Case of Hysteria* (1905).

Chapter Four (pp. 99-127)

Quotations in the text were taken from:

[Anonymous] *A Young Girl's Diary* (London: Unwin Hyman, 1990);

The Correspondence of Sigmund Freud and Sándor Ferenczi 1908-1914, Vol. 1 (Cambridge: The Belknap Press of Harvard University Press, 1994).

F. Ellenberger, *The Discovery of the Unconscious: The History and Evolution of Dynamic Psychiatry* (New York: Basic Books, 1970);

S. Freud, "Analysis of a Phobia in a Five-Year-Old Boy" (1909), in *The Standard Edition of the Complete Psychological Works of Sigmund Freud*, Vol. 10 (London: Hogarth Press, 1957).

S. Freud, "Notes upon a Case of Obsessional Neurosis" (1909), in *The Standard Edition of the Complete Psychological Works of Sigmund Freud*, Vol. 10 (London: Hogarth Press, 1957);

S. Freud, "Letter to Dr. Hermine von Hug-Hellmuth" (1919), in *The Standard Edition of the Complete Psychological Works of Sigmund Freud*, Vol. 14 (London: Hogarth Press, 1957), p. 341.

S. Freud, "An Autobiographical Study" (1925), in *The Standard Edition of the Complete Psychological Works of Sigmund Freud*, Vol. 20 (London: Hogarth Press, 1957);

S. Freud and L. Andreas-Salomé, *Letters* (New York: Norton, 1985);

The Freud/Jung Letters, ed. W. McGuire (London: Penguin, 1991);

P. Gay, *Freud: A Life for Our Time* (New York, London: Norton & Co., 1988);

P. Grosskurth, *Melanie Klein: Her World and Her Work* (New York: Hodder & Stoughton, 1986);

E. Jones, *Free Associations: Memoirs of a Psychoanalyst* (New York: Basic Books, 1959);

M. Kanzer and G. Glenn, *Preface*, in *Freud and His Patients* (New York: Jason Aronson, 1980, p. xiii);

P. Mahony, *Freud and the Rat Man* (New Haven and London: Yale Universities Press, 1986);

E. Roudinesco, *Jacques Lacan: Outline of a Life, History of a System of Thought* (New York: Columbia University Press, 1997);

W. Stekel, *Frigidity in Woman in Relation to Her Love Life*, Vol. 1 (New York: Grove Press, 1962), p. 176.

W. Stekel, *Patterns of Psychosexual Infantilism: Disorders of the Instincts and the Emotions. The Parapathiac Disorders* (New York: Grove Press, 1959), p. 308.

P. Sulloway, "Reassessing Freud's Clinical Case: The Social Construction of Psychoanalysis", *Isis*, 82 (1991), pp. 245-75.

On Hug-Hellmuth: G. MacLean and U. Rappen, *Hermine Hug-Hellmuth: Her Life and Work* (New York: Routledge 1991); L. Appignanesi and J. Forrester, *Freud's Women* (New York: Basic Books, 1992). See also D. Gunn and Patrick Guyomard (eds.), *A Young Girl's Diary* (London: Unwin Hyman, 1990), and S. Freud, "Letter to Dr Hermine von Hug-Hellmuth", in *The Standard Edition of the Complete Psychological Works of Sigmund Freud*, Vol. 14 (London: Hogarth Press, 1957), p. 341.

On Stekel: W. Stekel, *Autobiography* (New York: Liveright, 1950); E. Jones, *Free Associations. Memoirs of a Psychoanalyst* (New York: Basic Books, 1959); H. F. Ellenberger, *The Discovery of the Unconscious. The History and Evolution of Dynamic Psychiatry* (New York: Basic Books, 1970); P. Roazen, *Freud and his Followers*

(New York: Knopf, 1975); P. Gay, *Freud: A Life for our Time* (New York – London: Norton & Co., 1988). Freud's remarks were made in various letters to Ferenczi: see E. Brabant, E. Falzeder and P. Giampieri-Deutsch (eds.), *The Correspondence of Sigmund Freud and Sándor Ferenczi*, Vol. 1, *1908-1914*, trans. P. T. Hoffer, with introd. by A. Haynal (Cambridge, MA: The Belknap Press, 1993). See also S. Freud and L. Andreas-Salomé, *Letters* (New York: Harcourt Brace Jovanovich, 1972). The case of "Miss Anna" is described in W. Stekel, *Frigidity in Woman in Relation to Her Love Life*, trans. J. S. Van Teslaar, Vol. 1 (New York: Grove Press, 1962), p. 176. The case of the "Mirror Man" is described in W. Stekel, *Patterns of Psychosexual Infantilism. Disorders of the Instincts and the Emotions. The Parapathiac Disorders* (New York: Grove Press, 1959), p. 308.

The literature on Freud's clinical cases is increasing exponentially. A general overview may be found in the specific entries devoted to each clinical case in E. Roudinesco and M. Plon, *Dictionnaire de la psychanalyse* (Paris: Fayard, 1997) and A. de Mijolla (ed.), *International Dictionary of Psychoanalysis*, 3 vols. (Detroit: Thomson Gale, 2005). A remarkable critical analysis is provided by F. J. Sulloway, "Reassessing Freud's case histories. The social construction of psychoanalysis", *Isis*, 82, pp. 245-75. An orthodox position is expressed in K. Eissler, *Medical Orthodoxy and the Future of Psychoanalysis* (New York: International Universities Press, 1995).

On the case of "Anna O." (Bertha Pappenheim), see E. Breuer and S. Freud, "Studies on Hysteria", in *The Standard Edition of the Complete Psychological Works of Sigmund Freud*, Vol. 2; S. Freud, "An Autobiographical Study", in *The Standard Edition of the Complete Psychological Works of Sigmund Freud*, Vol. 20 (London: Hogarth Press, 1957); M. Borch-Jacobsen, *Remembering Anna O. A Century of Mystification* (London: Routledge, 1996).

On the case of "Rat Man" (Ernst Lanzer), see S. Freud, "Notes upon a Case of Obsessional Neurosis", in *The Standard Edition of the Complete Psychological Works of Sigmund Freud*, Vol. 10 (London: Hogarth Press, 1957), pp. 151-318; P. Mahony, *Freud and the Rat Man* (New Haven: Yale Universities Press, 1986). Mahony is the author of two other important works on Freud's cases, the case of "Dora" (*Freud's Dora*, New Haven: Yale University Press, 1996) and the case of "Wolf Man" (see chapter 5).

On the case of "Little Hans" (Herbert Graf), see S. Freud, "Analysis of a Phobia in a Five-Year-Old Boy", in *The Standard Edition of the Complete Psychological Works of Sigmund Freud*, Vol. 10 (London: Hogarth Press, 1957), pp. 1-149.

On the "case of Aimée" (Marguerite Anzieu) see E. Roudinesco, *Jacques Lacan. Outline of a Life, History of a System of Thought* (New York: Columbia University Press, 1997).

On the philological correctness of Freud's interpretations relative to etymologies, sources of slips, etc. see S. Timpanaro, *The Freudian Slip: Psychoanalysis and Textual Criticism* (London: NLB, 1974).

Chapter Five (pp. 128-46)

Quotations in the text were taken from:
F. Bassi, "Note sul caso clinico dell'uomo dei lupi", *Psicoterapia e Scienze Umane*, 1 (1992), pp. 38-63;
The Correspondence of Sigmund Freud and Sándor Ferenczi 1908-1914, Vol. 1 (Cambridge: The Belknap Press of Harvard University Press, 1994);
S. Freud, "From the History of an Infantile Neurosis" (1918), in *The Standard Edition of the Complete Psychological Works of Sigmund Freud*, Vol. 17 (London: Hogarth Press, 1957);

M. Gardiner (Ed.), *The Wolf-Man by the Wolf-Man* (New York: Basic Books, 1971);

E. Jones, *The Life and Work of Sigmund Freud*, Vol. 2 (New York: Basic Books, 1953);

L. Hellman, *Pentimento: A Book of Portraits* (London: Little, Brown, and Co., 2000);

P. J. Mahony, *Cries of the Wolf Man* (Chicago: The Chicago Institute of Psychoanalysis, 1984);

O. Mandelshtam, *Stone*, trans. R. Tracy (Princeton, N. J.: Princeton University Press, 1981);

K. Obholzer, *The Wolf-Man Sixty Years Later* (London: Routledge and Kegan Paul, 1982).

For the case of the Wolf Man (Sergey Pankeyev), see S. Freud, "From the History of an Infantile Neurosis" (1918) in *The Standard Edition of the Complete Psychological Works of Sigmund Freud*, Vol. 1, pp. 3-122 (London: Hogarth Press, 1957). The book *The Wolf Man by the Wolf Man*, ed. M. Gardiner (New York: Basic Books, 1971) contains an introduction by A. Freud, Freud's text of 1918, the "Memoirs of the Wolf Man", R. M. Brunswick's article of 1928 on this case, and Gardiner's own memoirs. Freud's famous letter to Ferenczi (February 13, 1910) appears in E. Brabant, E. Falzeder and P. Giampieri-Deutsch (eds.), *The Correspondence of Sigmund Freud and Sándor Ferenczi, 1908-1914*, Vol. I, trans. by P. T. Hoffer, with an introduction by A. Haynal, (Cambridge, MA: The Belknap Press of Harvard University Press, 1993). See also the "official" version in E. Jones, *Life and Works of Sigmund Freud* (New York: Basic Books, 1961). No one who wishes to understand this case can ignore the context of Russian culture: see J.L. Rice, *Freud's Russia: National Identity in the Evolution of Psychoanalysis* (New Brunswick and London: Transaction Publishers, 1993); A. Etkind, *Eros of the Impossible. The History of Psychoanalysis in Russia* (New York: Westview Press, 1997).

Other important studies include: N. Abraham and M. Torok, *The Wolf Man's Magic World* (Minneapolis: University of Minnesota Press, 1986); K. Obholzer, *The Wolf Man Sixty Years Later* (London: Routledge and Kegan Paul, 1982); P. J. Mahony, *Cries of the Wolf Man* (Chicago: The Chicago Institute of Psychoanalysis, 1984). For Rank's interpretation, see P. Grosskurth, *The Secret Ring: Freud's Inner Circle and the Politics of Psychoanalysis* (New York: Addison-Wesley, 1991). A critical analysis of the literature can be found in F. Bassi, "Note sul caso clinico dell'uomo dei lupi", *Psicoterapia e Scienze Umane*, 1 (1992), pp. 38-63.

On Muriel Gardiner, apart from the above-mentioned memoirs of the Wolf Man, see her autobiography *Code Name 'Mary': Memoirs of an American Woman in the Austrian Underground* (New Haven: Yale University Press, 1987) with a preface by A. Freud; L. Hellman, *Pentimento: A Book of Portraits* (London: Little Brown and Co., 2000); L. Appignanesi and J. Forrester, *Freud's Women* (New York: Basic Books, 1992).

The poem by Osip Mandelshtam appears in *Selected Poems*, trans. James Green (London: Penguin, 1991) and is referred to in A. Etkind, *Eros of the Impossible: The History of Psychoanalysis in Russia* (New York: Westview Press, 1997). Images of the headquarters of the Russian Society of Psychoanalysis and the Children House in Moscow are reproduced in my article "Casa Rjabusinskij", *Psicologia Contemporanea*, no. 147, 1998, pp. 14-16, or "Le Jardin Laboratoire de l'enfant de Moscou dans les années vingt", *Le Mouvement Psychoanalytique*, 9 (2009), pp. 115-9.

Chapter Six (pp. 147-52)

Quotations in the text were taken from:
E. Jablonsky, *Gershwin* (New York: Doubleday, 1987);

J. Peyser, *The Memory of All That: The Life of George Gershwin* (New York: Billboards, 1998).

For Gershwin's life, see E. Jablonsky, *Gershwin* (New York: Doubleday, 1987); J. Peyser, *The Memory of All That: The Life of George Gershwin* (New York: Billboards, 1998). For more specifically psychological and medical aspects, see S. Farber and M. Green, *Hollywood on the Couch: A Candid Look at the Overheated Love Affair between Psychiatrists and Moviemakers* (New York: Wlliam Morrow and Company, Inc., 1993), which examines the link with Zilboorg; A. Silverstein, "Neurologic History of George Gershwin", in *Mount Sinai Journal of Medicine*, Vol. 62 (1995), pp. 239-42.

On the question of brain tumours whose symptoms are mistaken for signs of personality disorders, see E.M. Aitken and PJ. Luce, "Frontal Lobe Tumours", *British Journal of Clinical Practice*, Vol. 50, 1996, pp. 339-41; M.S. Gazzaniga, R.B. Ivry and G.R. Mangun, *Cognitive Neuroscience. The Biology of Mind* (New York – London: Norton, 1998), p. 88.

Chapter Seven (pp. 153-74)

Quotations in the text were taken from:
S. Freud, "Thoughts for the Times on War and Death" (1915), in *The Standard Edition of the Complete Psychological Works of Sigmund Freud*, Vol. 14 (London: Hogarth Press, 1957);
S. Freud, "Mourning and Melancholia" (1917), both in *The Standard Edition of the Complete Psychological Works of Sigmund Freud*, Vol. 14 (London: Hogarth Press, 1957);
S. Freud, "Beyond the Principle of Pleasure" (1920), in *The Standard Edition of the Complete Psychological*

Works of Sigmund Freud, Vol. 18 (London: Hogarth Press, 1957);

P. Grosskurth, *Melanie Klein: Her World and Her Work* (New York: Hodder & Stoughton, 1986);

J. M. Masson, *The Assault on Truth: Freud's Suppression of the Seduction Theory* (New York: Farrar, Straus, and Giroux, 1904);

K. Obholzer, *The Wolf-Man Sixty Years Later* (London: Routledge and Kegan Paul, 1982);

P. Roazen, *Brother Animal: The Story of Freud and Tausk* (New York: New York Universities Press, 1969);

P. Roazen, *Freud and His Followers* (New York: Knopf, 1975);

N. Sutton, *Bruno Bettelheim: The Other Side of Madness* (London: George Duckworth, 1995);

E. Young-Bruehl, *Anna Freud: A Biography* (London: W. W. Norton, 1988).

Sigmund Freud's works on the issues analysed in this chapter are *Thoughts for the Times on War and Death* (1915) and *Mourning and Melancholia* (1917). Both appear in *The Standard Edition of the Complete Psychological Works* (Vol. 14).

For the presence of death in the life and work of Sigmund Freud, see M. Schur, *Freud: Living and Dying* (New York: International University Press, 1972); P. Gay, *Freud. A Life for Our Time* (New York – London: Norton, 1988).

On V. Tausk: P. Roazen, *Brother Animal: the Story of Freud and Tausk* (New York: New York Universities Press, 1969); K. Eissler, *Viktor Tausk's Suicide* (New York: International Universities Press, 1983); P. Roazen, *Helen Deutsch. A Psychoanalyst's Life* (New York: Anchor Press/ Doubleday 1985). Other important references: L. Andreas-Salomé, *The Freud Journal* (New York: Basic Books, 1964); S. Freud and Andreas-Salomé, *Letters* (London: Hogarth Press, 1972).

On L. Andreas-Salomé, see H. F. Peters, *My Sister, My Spouse. A Biography of Lou Andreas-Salomé* (New York: Norton, 1962).

On M. Klein's depression, see P. Grosskurth, *Melanie Klein: Her World and Her Work* (New York: Hodder & Stoughton, 1986).

On R. Mack Brunswick, see P. Roazen's works, *Freud and his Followers* (New York: Knopf, 1975) and *How Freud Worked. First-Hand Accounts of Patients* (Northwale, NJ: Jason Aronson Inc., 1995).

On R. Fliess, see J. M. Masson, *The Assault on Truth. Freud's Suppression of the Seduction Theory* (New York: Farrar, Straus, and Giroux, 1984).

On H. Silberer, see P. Roazen, *Freud and His Followers* (Harmondsworth: Penguin, 1979).

On B. Bettelheim, see N. Sutton, *Bruno Bettelheim. The Other Side of Madness* (London: George Duckworth, 1995). See also P. Roazen, "The Rise and Fall of Bruno Bettelheim", *Psychohistory Review*, 20 (1992), pp. 221-49.

On P. Theiler, see W. Boelich (ed.), *The Letters of Sigmund Freud to Eduard Silberstein, 1871-1881* (Cambridge, MA: Belknap Press 1990).

On the high frequency of suicides among psychoanalysts see P. Roazen, *Freud and His Followers* (Harmondsworth: Penguin, 1979); and the entries relating to various psychoanalysts and the entry for "Suicide" in E. Roudinesco and M. Pion, *Dictionnaire de la psychanalyse* (Paris: Fayard, 1997).

Epilogue (pp. 175-80)

Quotations in the text are from:
B. Bettelheim, *A Home for the Heart* (New York: Knopf, 1974), p. 284.

S. Freud, "Recommendations to Physicians Practising Psycho-Analysis" (1912), and "Analysis Terminable and Interminable" (1937), both in *The Standard Edition of the Complete Psychological Works*, Vol. 12 (London: Hogarth Press, 1957).

S. Freud, "Analysis Terminable and Interminable" (1937), in *The Standard Edition of the Complete Psychological Works*, Vol. 23. (London: Hogarth Press, 1957).

G. Jervis, *La psicoanalisi come esercizio critico* (Milan: Garzanti, 1989), p. 60.

On Tom Seidmann-Freud, see B. Murken, "Tom Seidmann-Freud: Leben und Werk. Die Schiefertafel", *Zeitschrift für historische Kinderbuchforschung*, 4 (1981), pp. 163-201, and the catalogue edited by Barbara Murken for the exhibition of books by Freud's niece, organised in 1984 by the Institut für Jugendbuchforschung in Frankfurt (I would like to thank the Institute's library for kindly having sent me a copy of this precious little book). There is also a reference to Tom in G. Scholem, *Von Berlin nach Jerusalem. Jugenderinnerungen* (Frankfurt: Suhrkamp, 1977).

The B. Bettelheim quotation is taken from his book *A Home for the Heart* (New York: Knopf, 1974), p. 284.

The literature on the methodological flaws of psychoanalysis is expanding. A good introductory work is M.S. Roth (ed.), *Freud: Conflict and Culture* (New York: Knopf, 1998), which includes two interesting chapters by F. Cioffi and A. Grünbaum summarising the two different perspectives on the scientific validity of psychoanalysis (the "biographical" and the "theoretical"). For a more detailed analysis, see F. Cioffi, *Freud and the Question of Pseudo-Science* (Chicago: Open Court, 1998) and A. Grünbaum, *The Foundations of Psychoanalysis,* Berkeley: University of California Press, 1984).

The G. Jervis quotation is taken from his book, *La psicoanalisi come esercizio critico* (Milan: Garzanti, 1989), p. 60.

Index

Index

206

Other Vagabonds Other Vagabonds Other Vagabonds Other Vagabonds

Allan Cameron's **In Praise of the Garrulous**

About the book

This first work of non-fiction by the author of *The Golden Menagerie* and *The Berlusconi Bonus*, has an accessible and conversational tone, which perhaps disguises its enormous ambition. The writer examines the history of language and how it has been affected by technology, primarily writing and printing. This leads to some important questions concerning the "ecology" of language, and how any degradation it suffers might affect "not only our competence in organising ourselves socially and politically, but also our inner selves."

Comments

"A deeply reflective, extraordinarily wide-ranging meditation on the nature of language, infused in its every phrase by a passionate humanism" – Terry Eagleton

"This is a brilliant tour de force, in space and in time, into the origins of language, speech and the word. ... Such a journey into the world of the word needs an articulate and eloquent guide: Allan Cameron is both and much more than that." – Ilan Pappé

I like *In Praise of the Garrulous* very much indeed, not only because it says a good many interesting and true things, but because of its *tone* and style. Its combination of personal passion, observation, stories, poetic bits and serious expert argument, expressed as it is in the prose of an intelligent conversation: all this is ideal for holding and persuading intelligent but non-expert readers. In my opinion he has done nothing better." – Eric Hobsbawm.

Price: £8.00   ISBN: 978-0-9560560-0-9   In print

Allan Massie's **Surviving**

About the book

Surviving is set in contemporary Rome. The main characters, Belinda, Kate (an author who specialises in studies of the criminal mind, and Tom Durward (a scriptwriter), attend an English-speaking group of Alcoholics Anonymous. All have pasts to cause embarrassment or shame. Tom sees no future for himself and still gets nervous "come Martini time". Belinda embarks on a love-affair that cannot last. Kate ventures onto more dangerous ground by inviting her latest case-study, a young Londoner acquitted of a racist murder, to stay with her.

Allan Massie dissects this group of ex-pats in order to say something about our inability to know, still less to understand, the actions of our fellow human beings, even when relationships are so intense. It is also, therefore, impossible or at least difficult to make informed moral judgements of others. This is an intelligent book that examines human nature with a deft and light touch.

Comments

A Question of Loyalties: "Brilliant novel, taking in the whole agony of Europe" – Auberon Waugh in *The Independent*

The Sins of the Father: "A marvellous read, dealing with big themes in an original and striking way" – Nicholas Mosley (*Daily Telegraph* Books of the Year)

Shadows of Empire: "An important work. It grips from start to finish." – Muriel Spark

These Enchanted Woods: "Very observant, very funny, and very enjoyable" – William Dalrymple in *The Daily Mail*

Price: £10.00   ISBN: 978-0-9560560-0-9   Publication date: 8.6.09